Six Modern Women

Six Modern Women

Laura M. Hasson

Z & L Barnes Publishing

CONTENTS

It is not my purpose to contribute to the study of woman's intellectual life, or to discuss her capacity for artistic production, although these six women are in a manner representative of woman's intellect and woman's creative faculty. I have little to do with Marie Bashkirtseff's pictures in the Luxembourg, Sonia Kovalevsky's doctor's degree and *Prix Bordin*, Anne Charlotte Edgren-Leffler's stories and social dramas, Eleonora Duse's success as a tragedian in both worlds, and with all that has made their names famous and is publicly known about them. There is only one point which I should like to emphasize in these six types of modern womanhood, and that is the manifestation of their womanly feelings. I want to show how it asserts itself in spite of everything,—in spite of the theories on which they built up their lives, in spite of the opinions of which they were the teachers, and in spite of the success which crowned their efforts, and bound them by stronger chains than might have been the case had their lives been passed in obscurity. They were out of harmony with themselves, suffering from a conflict which made its first appearance in the world when the "woman question" came to the fore, causing an unnatural breach between the needs of the intellect and the requirements of their womanly nature. Most of them succumbed in the struggle.

A woman who seeks freedom by means of the modern method of independence is generally one who desires to escape from a woman's sufferings. She is anxious to avoid subjection, also motherhood, and the dependence and impersonality of an ordinary woman's life; but in doing so she unconsciously deprives herself of her womanliness. For them all—for Marie Bashkirtseff as much as Sonia Kovalevsky and A.

C. Edgren-Leffler—the day came when they found themselves standing at the door of the heart's innermost sanctuary, and realized that they were excluded. Some of them burst open the door, entered, and became man's once more. Others remained outside and died there. They were all individualistic, these six women. It was this fact that molded their destiny; but Eleonora Duse was the only one of them who was individualistic enough. None of them were able to stand alone, as more than one had believed that she could. The women of our day are difficult in the choice of a husband, and the men are slow and mistrustful in their search for a wife.

There are some hidden peculiarities in woman's soul which I have traced in the lives of these six representative women, and I have written them down for the benefit of those who have not had the opportunity of discovering them for themselves.

The subjects of these six psychological sketches are well known to English readers, with the exception of Amalie Skram, the Norwegian novelist, and Fru Leffler, who is known only as the biographer of Sonia Kovalevsky.

Laura Marholm, the writer of this book, is a German authoress of Norwegian extraction, who is celebrated for her literary criticisms and the beauty of her style. In September, 1889, she married Ola Hansson, the Swedish author of "Sensitiva Amorosa," "Young Scandinavia," and a novel called "Fru Esther Bruce," in which the heroine is said to bear a strong resemblance to Eleonora Duse. He has also published a volume of prose poems, called "Ofeg's Ditties," which has been translated by George Egerton, whose vivid style and powerful descriptions have gained a place for her among the foremost women writers of the day.

Laura Marholm was the first to introduce her husband to the German public by means of two articles in the *Neue Freie Presse*. The first, called "A Swedish Love Poet," appeared May 24th, 1888, before they had met, and was written in praise of his early work, "Sensitiva Amorosa." The second article was a criticism on "Pariahs," and it is an interesting fact that in it she compares him to Gottfried Keller.

In all her writings, Laura Marholm looks at life through the spectacles of a happy marriage; she believes that matured thought and widened views can—in a woman's case—be only the direct result of marriage; and consequently she considers marriage to be absolutely indispensable to every woman, and that without it she is both mentally and morally undeveloped. She has little sympathy with the Woman's Rights movement, judged either from the social, political, or educational point of view; with regard to the latter, she has not had a university education herself, and she is not at all impressed by those who have. She considers that a woman's individuality is of greater importance than her actions; she upholds woman's influence *as woman*, and has no sympathy with the advanced thinkers, who, with Stuart Mill at their head, would fain have women exert their influence as thinking, reasoning human beings, believing all other influence to be unworthy the dignity of the modern woman. Laura Marholm has the intuitive faculty, and this enables her to gauge the feelings of those women who spend a long youth in waiting—who are taught to believe, and who do believe, that their youth is nothing more than a transition period between childhood and marriage,—women who grow old in waiting, and awake to reality to find behind them nothing but a wasted youth, and in the future—an empty old age. But these are not modern women, they are the women of the *ancien régime*, who have missed their vocation, and failed to attain their sole object in life,—viz., marriage. On the one hand we are confronted with the old-fashioned girl, on the other by the new woman. Of the two, we prefer the new woman; and while recognizing her mistakes, and lamenting her exaggerated views, Laura Marholm acknowledges that she is formed of the best material of the age, and prophesies for her a brighter future. But her views differ greatly from those of Ibsen and Björnson. According to Ibsen, a woman is first of all a human being, and then a woman; she places the woman first, the human being last. Björnson believes that an intellectually developed woman with a life-work can get on very well by herself; Laura Marholm maintains that, apart from man, a woman is nothing. According to her, woman is a creature of instinct, and this instinct is her most precious possession, and of far greater value than the intellect. Of all the studies in this book, Fru Leffler is probably the one with whom she is least in sympathy. Fru Leffler was essentially intellectual, possessed of a some-what cold and critical temperament, and in writing the biography of Sonia Kovalevsky she was often unable to appreciate the latter's very complicated character. Sonia was a rare combination of the mystic and the scientist; she was not only a mathematician, but also, in every important crisis of her life, a dreamer of prophetic dreams. The biography was intended to be the continuation of Sonia's own story of her childhood, and the two should be read together. As a child, Sonia suffered from a painful conviction that in her family she was not the favorite, and it is probable that her unaccountable shyness, her want of self-confidence, and her inability to attract love in after life, were due to the fact of her having passed an unhappy and unloved childhood.

Fru Leffler's writings are remarkable for the simplicity and directness of her style, her keen observation, and love of truth. Her talents were by no means confined to her pen; she held a salon,—the resort of the intellectual world of Stockholm,—and attained great popularity by her tactfulness and social gifts. She did not, however, shine in society to the same extent as Sonia Kovalevsky. Her conversation was not as brilliant and witty as the latter's, but it was always interesting, and it was of the kind that is remembered long afterwards. "When she told a story, analyzed a psychological problem, or recounted the contents of a book, she always succeeded in setting forth its real character in a clear and decided manner." Sonia, on the other hand, was ever ready with an original remark. Ellen Key tells how one day, when the conversation turned upon love, Sonia exclaimed: "These amiable young men are always writing books about love, and they do not even know that some people have a genius for loving, just as others have a genius for music and mechanics, and that for these erotic geniuses love is a matter of life and death, whereas for others it is only an episode."

Fru Leffler travelled a great deal, and made many friends in the countries that she visited. She took great interest in socialism, anarchism, and all religious and educational movements. In London she attended lectures given by Mrs. Marx-Aveling, Bradlaugh, and Mrs. Besant. Theosophy, positivism, spiritualism, and atheism,—there was nothing which did not interest her. The more she saw the more she doubted the possibility of attaining to absolute truth in matters either social or religious, and the more attracted she became by the doctrine of evolution.

From this authoress, who was the chief exponent of woman's rights in Sweden, we turn to a very different but no less interesting type. Eleonora Duse, the great Italian actress, has visited London during the past few years, acting in such a natural, and at the same time in such a simple and life-like manner, that a knowledge of the language was not absolutely indispensable to the enjoyment of the piece. Besides most of the pieces mentioned here, she acted in *La Femme de Claude, Cleopatra*, and *Martha*; but she attained her greatest triumph in Goldoni's comedy, *La Locandiera*.

In all these typical women, Fru L. Marholm Hansson traces a likeness which proves that they have something in common. Numerous and conflicting as are the various opinions on the so-called "woman question," the best, and perhaps the only, way of elucidating it is by doing as she has done in giving us these sketches. We have here six modern women belonging to five nationalities, three of whom are authoresses, and the other three—mathematician, actress, and artist, portrayed and criticized by one who is herself a modern woman and an authoress.

H. R.

The Learned Woman

1

It sometimes happens that a hidden characteristic of the age is disclosed, not through any acuteness on the part of the spectator, nor as the result of critical research, but of itself, as it were, and spontaneously. A worn face rises before us, bearing the marks of death, and never again may we gaze into the eyes which reveal the deep psychological life of the soul. It is the dead who greet us, the dead who survive us, and who will come to life again and again in future generations, long after we have ceased to be; those dead who will become the living, only to suffer and to die again.

These self-revelations have always existed amongst men, but among women they were unknown until now, when this tired century is drawing to its close. It is one of the strangest signs of the coming age that woman has attained to the intellectual consciousness of herself as woman, and can say what she is, what she wishes, and what she longs for. But she pays for this knowledge with her death.

Marie Bashkirtseff's Journal was just such a self-revelation as this; the moment it appeared it was carried throughout the whole of Europe, and further than Europe, on far-reaching waves of human sympathy. Wherever it went it threw a firebrand into the women's hearts, which set them burning without most of them knowing what this burning betokened. They read the book with a strange and painful emotion, for as they turned over these pages so full of ardent energy, tears, and yearning, they beheld their own selves, strange, beautiful, and exalted, but still themselves, though few of them could have explained why or wherefore.

It was no bitter struggle with the outer world to which Marie Bashkirtseff succumbed at the age of four-and-twenty; it was not the struggle of a girl of the middle classes for her daily bread, for which she sacrifices her youth and spirits; she met with no obstacles beyond the traditional customs which had become to her a second nature, no obstruction greater than the atmosphere of the age in which she lived, which bounded her own horizon, although in her inmost soul she rebelled against it. She had everything that the world can give to assist the unhindered development of the inner life,—mental, spiritual, and physical; everything that hundreds of thousands of women, whose narrow lives need expanding, have not got,—and yet she did not live her life. On every one of the six hundred pages of her journal (written, as it is, in her penetrating Russian-French style) we meet the despairing cry that she had nothing, that she was ever alone in the midst of an ever-lasting void, hungering at the table of life, spread for every one except herself, standing with hands outstretched as the days passed by and gave her nothing; youth and health were fading fast, the grave was yawning, just a little chink, then wider and wider, and she must go down without having had anything but work,—constant work,—trouble and striving, and the empty fame which gives a stone in the place of bread.

*****

The tired and discontented women of the time recognized them-selves on every page, and for many of them Marie Bashkirtseff's Journal became a kind of secret Bible in which they read a few sentences every morning, or at night before going to sleep.

A few years later there appeared another confession by a woman; this time it was not an autobiography, like the last one, but it was written by a friend, who was a European celebrity, with a name as lasting as her own. This book was called "Sonia Kovalevsky: Our Mutual Experiences, and the things she told me about herself." The writer was Anne Charlotte Edgren-Leffler, Duchess of Cajanello, who had been her daily companion during years of friendship.

There was a curious likeness between Marie Bashkirtseff's Journal and Sonia Kovalevsky's confessions, something in their innermost, personal experiences which proves an identity of temperament as well as of fortune, something which was not only due to the unconscious manner in which they criticized life, but to life itself, life as they molded it, and as each was destined to live it. Marie Bashkirtseff and Sonia Kovalevsky were both Russians,[1] both descended from rich and noble families, both women of genius, and from their earliest childhood they were both in a position to obtain all the advantages of a good education. They were both born rulers, true children of nature, full of originality, proud and independent. In all respects they were the favorites of fortune, and yet —and yet neither of these extraordinary women was satisfied, and they died because they could not be satisfied. Is not this a sign of the times?

2

The story of Sonia Kovalevsky's life reads like an exciting novel, which is, if anything, too richly furnished with strange events. Such is life. It comes with hands full to its chosen ones, but it also takes away gifts more priceless than it gave.

At the age of eighteen Sonia Kovalevsky was already the mistress of her own fate. She had married the husband of her choice, and he had accompanied her to Heidelberg, where they both matriculated at the university. From thence he took her to Berlin, where she lived with a girl friend, who was a student like herself, and studied mathematics at Weierstrass's for the space of four years, only meeting her husband occasionally in the course of her walks. Her marriage with Valdemar Kovalevsky, afterwards Professor of Paleontology at the university of Moscow, was a mere formality, and this extraordinary circumstance brings us face to face with one of the chief characteristics of her nature.

Sonia Kovalevsky did not love her husband; there was, in fact, nothing in her early youth to which she was less disposed than love. She was possessed of an immense undefined thirst, which was something more than a thirst for study, albeit that was the form which it took. Her inexperienced, child-like nature was weighed down beneath the burden of an exceptional talent.

Sonia Krukovsky was the daughter of General Krukovsky of Palibino, a French Grand-seigneur of old family; and when she was no more than sixteen, she had in her the making of a great mathematician and a great authoress. She was fully aware of the first, but of the latter she knew nothing, for a woman's literary talent nearly always dates its origin from her experience of life. She was high-spirited and enterprising,—qualities which are more often found among the Sclavonic women than any other race of Europeans; she had that peculiar consciousness of the shortness of life, the same which drove Marie Bashkirtseff to accomplish more in the course of a few years than most people would have achieved during the course of their whole existence.

Sonia Kovalevsky's girlhood was spent in Russia, during those years of feverish excitement when the outbreaks of the Nihilists bore witness to the working of a subterranean volcano, and the hearts and intellects of the young glowed with an enthusiasm which led to the self-annihilating deeds of fanaticism. A few winter months spent at St. Petersburg decided the fate of Sonia and her elder sister, Anjuta. The strict, old-fashioned notions of their family allowed them very little liberty, and they longed for independence. In order to escape from parental authority, a formal marriage was at this time a very favorite expedient among young girls in Russia. A silent but widespread antagonism reigned in all circles between the old and young; the latter treated one another as secret allies, who by a look or pressure of the hand could make themselves understood. It was not at all uncommon for a girl to propose a formal marriage to a young man, generally with the purpose of studying abroad, as this was the only means by which they could obtain the consent of their unsuspecting parents to undertake the journey. When they were abroad, they generally released each other from all claims and separated, in order to study apart. Sonia's sister was anxious to escape in this way, as she possessed a remarkable literary talent which her father had forbidden her to exercise. She accordingly made the proposal in question to a young student of good family, named Valdemar Kovalevsky; he, however, preferred Sonia, and this gave rise to further complications, as their father refused to allow the younger sister to marry before the elder.

Sonia resorted to a stratagem, and one evening, when her parents were giving a reception, she went secretly to Valdemar, and as soon as her absence was discovered she sent a note to her father, with these words: "I am with Valdemar; do not oppose our marriage any longer." There remained no alternative for General Krukovsky but to fetch his daughter home as speedily as possible, and to announce her engagement.

They were accompanied on their honeymoon by a girl friend, who was equally imbued with the desire to study, and soon afterwards Anjuta joined them. The first thing that Sonia and Valdemar did was to visit George Eliot in London; after which Valdemar went to Jena and Munich, while Sonia, with her sister and friend, studied at Heidelberg, where they remained during two terms before going to Berlin. The sister went secretly to Paris by herself.

Arrived at Berlin, Sonia buried herself in her work. She saw no one except Professor Weierstrass, who expressed the greatest admiration for her quickness at mathematics, and did all in his power to assist her by means of private lessons. If we are honest enough to call it by its true name, we must confess that the life led by these two girls, during eight terms, was the life of a dog. Sonia scarcely ever went out of doors unless Valdemar fetched her for a walk, which was not often, as he lived in another part of the town, and was constantly away. She was tormented with a vague fear of exposing herself. Inexperienced as both these friends were, they lived poorly, and ate little, allowing themselves no pleasure of any sort, added to which they were tyrannized over and cheated by their maid-servant. Sonia sat all day long at her writing-table, hard at work with her mathematical exercises; and when she took a short rest, it was only to run up and down the room, talking aloud to herself, with her brains as busy as ever. She had never been accustomed to do anything for herself; she had always been waited upon, and it was impossible to persuade her even to buy a dress when necessary, unless Valdemar accompanied her. But Valdemar soon tired of rendering these unrequited services, and he often absented himself in other towns for the completion of his own studies; and as they both received an abundant supply of money from their respective homes, they were in no way dependent upon each other.

The year 1870 came and went; for Sonia it had been a year of study, and nothing more. Her sleep had become shorter and more broken, and she neither knew nor cared what she ate, when suddenly, in the spring of the following year, she was sent for by her sister in Paris. Anjuta had fallen passionately in love with a young Parisian, who was a member of the Commune; he had just been arrested, and was in danger of losing his life. Sonia and Valdemar succeeded in penetrating through the line of troops, found Anjuta, and wrote to their father. General Krukovsky came at once, and it was only then that he discovered what his daughters were doing abroad, and learned for the first time that his eldest daughter had been living alone in Paris, for Anjuta had always been careful to send her letters through Sonia, with the Berlin postmark.

Anjuta showed great spirit, and after an interview with Thiers they succeeded in helping this very undesirable son-in-law to escape. Throughout the whole affair their father's behavior is a rare proof of the nobility of the race from which Sonia sprang. This stern man not only forgave—he also admired his daughters for what they had done. The cold manner and grandfatherly authority with which he had hitherto treated them was superseded by a cordial sympathy such as would have been impossible before. He was much impressed by Anjuta's passion, but Sonia's platonic marriage distressed him greatly.

In the year 1874 Sonia took the degree of doctor at Göttingen, as the result of three mathematical treatises, of which one especially, her thesis "On the Theory of Partial Differential Equations," is reckoned one of her most prominent works. Immediately after this, the whole family assembled on the old estate of Palibino. Sonia was completely worn out, and it was a long time before she was able to resume any severe brain work. Her holiday was cut short by her father's death a few months later, and the following winter was spent with her family at St. Petersburg. Until now Sonia's brain was the only part of her which was thoroughly awakened. She had been entirely absorbed in her studies, and had worked with the obstinate tenacity of auto-suggestion, more commonly found in women, especially girls, than in men. Marie Bashkirtseff had done the same, year in, year out; she had worked breathlessly, feverishly, with an incomprehensible, unwearied power of production,—while failing health was announcing the approach of death in her frail young body. Suddenly the end came.

Thousands of girls in middle-class families work themselves to death in the same way. Badly paid to begin with, they lower the prices still more by competing with one another. Others, placed in better circumstances, work with the same insistency at useless handicrafts, while a large number of women of the poorer classes work because they are driven to it by dire necessity. The result is the same in all cases; they lose the power of enjoyment, and forget what happiness means.

Sonia's stay in St. Petersburg was the occasion of the first great change which took place in her, to be followed later on by many like changes. Mathematics were thrust aside; she did not want to hear any more about them, she wanted to forget them.

Mind and body were undergoing a healing process, struggling to attain an even balance in her fresh young nature. She felt the need of change, she required companionship, and she threw herself into the midst of all social and intellectual pursuits. It was then that the woman awoke in her.

During the period of nervous excitement and sorrow which followed after the death of her beloved father, she had become the wife of her husband, after having been nominally married for nearly seven years. Since then they had drawn closer to one another; and now that her fortune, as long as her mother lived, was not sufficient for her support, she and Valdemar invested their money in various speculations. With true Russian enthusiasm they set to work building houses, establishing watering-places, and starting newspapers, besides lending their aid to every imaginable kind of new invention. The first year all went well, and in 1878 a daughter was born. After that came the crash. Kovalevsky was bitten with the rage for speculation, and although he was nominated Professor of Paleontology at Moscow in 1880, and in spite of all that his wife could do to dissuade him, he took shares in a company connected with petroleum springs in the south of Russia. The company was a swindle, the undertaking proved a failure, and he shot himself.

Sonia had left him some time before. She knew what was coming, having been warned by bad dreams and presentiments, and as she had lost her influence over him, and was anxious to provide for her own and her child's future, she left him and went to Paris. Just as she was recovering from the nervous fever to which she succumbed on hearing the news of her husband's sudden death, she received the summons to go to Stockholm.

The invitation had been sent by the representatives of a Woman's Rights movement which was then in full swing. It was an exceedingly narrow society of the genuine *bourgeois* kind, and as it was to them that she owed her appointment, they were anxious to bind her firmly to their cause. Sonia soon won their hearts by the sociability of her Russian nature, but as one term after the other passed by, she grew more and more weary of it, and whenever her course of lectures was over she hurried away as quickly as possible to Russia, Italy, France, England,—no matter where, if only she could escape out of Sweden into a freer atmosphere. She never looked upon her stay there as anything more than an episode in her life, and she longed to be back in Paris; but the years passed by, and she received no other appointment.

Her lectures at the university began to pall upon her; it gave her no pleasure to be forever teaching the students the same thing in a dreary routine. She needed an incentive in the shape of some highly gifted individual whom she could respect, and whose presence would call forth her highest faculties; but even the esteem in which she held some few people was not of long duration.

Her friendship with Fru Edgren-Leffler dates from this period. It was this lady's renown as an authoress which roused Sonia's talent for writing, for her life had been rich in experiences, and never wanting in variety until now, when, in a period of comparative leisure, she allowed her thoughts to dwell upon the past. She began by persuading Fru Edgren-Leffler to dramatize the sketches which she gave her, and "The Struggle for Happiness" was the first result of this collaboration. But Sonia soon realized that the honest, simple-minded Swede was not in sympathy with this department of literature; so she wrote a story on her own account, entitled "The Sisters Rajevsky," which was a sketch of her own youth, followed by an excellent novel called "Vera Barantzova;" after which she began another novel called "Vae Victis," which was never finished.

3

Up till now we have followed this remarkable woman's life along a clear, though somewhat agitated course; but from henceforward there is something uncomfortable, something strange and distorted about it. It is very difficult for us to ascertain the cause of her increasing distraction of mind, and early death, and the difficulty is intensified by the fact that the material contributed by Fru Leffler is poor and contradictory, and also because her work is disfigured by the peculiar inferences which she draws.

I have seen four portraits of Sonia Kovalevsky, and they are all so entirely different that no one would imagine that they were intended to represent the same person. She had none of the fascinating, though irregular beauty of Marie Bashkirtseff, who carried on an artistic cult with her own person. Sonia's powerful head, with the short hair, massive forehead, and short-sighted eyes of the color of "green gooseberries in syrup," was placed on a delicate child-like body. Her chief charm lay in her extraordinary liveliness and habit of giving herself up entirely to the interest of the moment; but she was completely unversed in the art of dress, and did not know how to appear at her best; she never gave any thought to the subject at all until she was thirty; and although she paid more attention to it then, she never learned the secret. She aged early, and a celebrated poet has described her to me as being a withered little old woman at the age of thirty. These external circumstances stood more in her way in Sweden, among a tall, fair people, than would have been possible either in Russia or in Paris. Between herself and the Swedish type there was a wide gulf fixed, which allowed no encouragement to the finer erotic emotions to which she was very strongly disposed; she felt crushed, and her impressionable, unattractive nature suffered acutely from being so unlike the ordinary victorious type of beauty. The picture of her when she was eighteen bears a strong resemblance to the late King Louis II. of Bavaria; not only are her features like his, but also the expression in the eyes and the curve of the lips. The second picture dates from the year 1887. It has something wearied and disillusioned about it, and she seems to be making an effort to appear amiable. It was taken at the time when she was struggling to accustom herself to the stiff, prudish, and somewhat pretentious ways of Stockholm society. The third portrait was taken at the time when she won the *Prix Bordin* in Paris, and it is a regular Russian face, with a much more cheerful expression than the former ones. But in the last picture, taken in the year 1890, which was, to a certain extent, official and very much touched up, how ill she looks; how disappointed and how weary! These four portraits are, to my mind, four different women; they show us what Sonia was once, and what she became after living for several years in an uncongenial atmosphere.

Sonia Kovalevsky was a true Russian genius, with an elastic nature. She was lavish and careless in her ways, and she thrived best upon a torn sofa in an atmosphere of tea, cigarettes, and profusion of all kinds,—intellectual, spiritual, and pecuniary; she needed to be surrounded by people like herself, who were in sympathy with her, and the inhabitants of Stockholm were never that. She had been torn away from the Russian surroundings in which she had lived in Berlin. She, who never could endure solitude, found herself alone among strangers, who forced themselves upon her,—hard, angular, women's rights women, who expected her to be their leader, and to fulfil a mission. She seldom rebelled against the duties which were constantly held before her eyes, partly because her vanity was flattered by the public position which she occupied, and also because her livelihood depended upon it, now that her private means were not sufficient for her support, and for the numerous journeys which she undertook.

A great deal of her time was spent in travelling to and fro between Stockholm and St. Petersburg, where she went to visit Anjuta, whose marriage had turned out most unhappily, and who was suffering from a severe illness, of which she afterwards died. After her sister's death Sonia took a great interest in the study of Northern literature, which was then just beginning to attract attention. She also wrote books, and solved some mathematical problems. Every time that she returned to Stockholm, after spending her holidays in Russia or the South, she had almost entirely forgotten her Swedish, and every year that passed by called forth fresh lamentations over her exile. The tone of society in Stockholm was unendurable to her; but she was of too disciplined a character, and too gentle, too submissive in her loneliness, to rebel against it. Her life became monotonous, which it had never been before, and her courage began to give way. She yearned for sympathy, for excitement, for her native land,—for everything, in fact, which was denied her.

She also longed for something else, which was the very thing that she could not have. She was seized with an eager, nervous longing to be loved. She wanted to be a woman, to possess a woman's charm. She had lived like a widow for years during her husband's lifetime, and for years after his death as well. As long as her mathematical studies produced a tension in her mind, she asked for nothing better, but buried herself in her work, and was perfectly contented. When she started being an authoress, a change came over her character. The development of the imagination created a need for love, and because this devouring need could not be satisfied, she became exacting, discontented, and mistrustful of the amount of affection which was accorded her. In her younger days she had asked for nothing more than that curious kind of mystic love, known only to Russians, which had run its course in mutual enthusiasm of a purely intellectual and spiritual character. It was otherwise now. She lamented her lost youth, and the time wasted in study; she regretted the unfortunate talent which had deprived her womanhood of its attractiveness. She wanted to be a woman, and to enjoy life as a woman.

She had also another wish, just as passionate in its way and as difficult of fulfilment as the former one, and this was her wish to receive an appointment in Paris. It was to a certain extent fulfilled when she was awarded the *Prix Bordin* on Christmas Eve, 1888, on the occasion of a solemn session of the French Academy of Science, in an assembly which was largely composed of learned men. It was the highest scientific distinction which had ever been accorded to a woman, and from henceforth she was an European celebrity, with a place in history. But it gave her no pleasure. She was as completely knocked up as she had been after receiving her doctor's degree. She had worked day and night for days beforehand, and during the weeks that followed she took part in the social functions which were given in her honor. She left no pleasure untasted, and yet she was not satisfied, for by this time her yearning for love had reached its highest pitch.

A short time before, Sonia had made the acquaintance of a cousin of her late husband's, "fat M.," as she called him. The companionship of a sympathetic fellow-countryman put her in the height of good humor, and she soon found it so indispensable that she wanted to have him always at her side, and was never happy except when he was there. M. K. did not return this strong affection; he was, however, quite willing to marry her, and the result was that a most unfortunate relationship sprang up between them. Sonia could not exist without him, so they travelled from Stockholm to Russia, and from Russia to Paris or Italy, in order to spend a few weeks together, and then separated, because by that time they were mutually tired of each other. It was on one of these journeys, when Sonia had come out of the sunshine of Italy into the winter of Sweden, that she caught cold, and no sooner had she arrived at Stockholm than she did everything to make her condition worse. In a desperate mood of indifference she immediately commenced her lectures, and went to all the social entertainments that were given. Dark presentiments and dreams, in which she always believed, had foretold that this year would be fatal to her. Longing for death, yet fearing it, she died suddenly in the beginning of the year 1891.

4

Those who know something about Russian women, without having any very detailed knowledge, divide them into two types, and a superficial observer would class Sonia Kovalevsky as belonging to one or the other of these. The first type consists of luxurious, languishing, idle, fascinating women, with passionate black eyes, or playful gray ones, a soft skin, and a delicate mouth, which is admirably adapted for laughing and eating. These women have a most seductive charm; their movements suggest that they are wont to recline on soft pillows, dressed *en négligé*, and their power of chattering is unlimited, and varies in tone from the most enchanting flattery to the worst temper imaginable. They are, in fact, the most womanly of women, as little to be depended upon in their amiability as in their anger; they are quick to fall in love, and men are as quickly enthralled by them. But Sonia Kovalevsky was not one of these.

The women of the second type present the greatest contrast that it is possible to imagine. They are honest and straightforward, and essentially what is called "a good fellow," plain, sensible, brave, energetic, as strong in soul as in body,—thinking heads, flat figures; they have none of that grace of form which is peculiar to a large number of Russian women. Their faces are generally sallow, and their skin is clammy, but thoroughly Russian in spite of it. There is something lacking in them, which for want of a better expression I shall call a want of sweetness. There is a curious neutrality about them; it takes one some time to realize that they are women. And they themselves are but dimly conscious of it, and then only on rare occasions. They are generally people with a mission,—working people, people with ideas.

It is these women who have furnished the largest contingent to the ranks of the Nihilists. It is they who chose to lead the lives of hunted wild beasts, and who found ample compensation in mental excitement for all that they had renounced as women and as persons of refinement. But although this last is a genuine Russian type, it is by no means confined to Russia. It is a type peculiar to the age. The class of women who become Nihilists in Russia are the champions for women's rights in Sweden, and it is they who agitate for women's franchise in England, who start women's clubs in America, and become governesses in Germany.

The type is universal, but it is left to circumstances to decide which special form of mania it is to take,—a form of mania which calls itself "a vocation in life." In Russia the woman, in whom sex lay dormant, felt it her calling to become a murderess, and that merely from a general desire to promote the popular welfare; in Germany this philanthropic spirit took the form of wishing to prune little human plants in the Kindergarten. But this is a long chapter, which I cannot pursue any further at present, and which, like many others on the characteristics of the woman of to-day, I shall keep for a separate book. We must include Sonia Kovalevsky in this latter type: she considered herself as belonging to it, and the whole course of her life is in itself sufficient to prove that she was one of them. The nature of her friendships with men furnishes us with yet another proof. She had a large circle of acquaintances, amongst whom were some of the best known and most talented men of Russia, Scandinavia, England, Germany, France, and Italy,—all of whom enjoyed her society, although not one of them fell in love with her, and not one among those thousands said to her, "I cannot exist without you."

She belonged to the class of women with brains, and she was numbered amongst them. She was their triumphant banner, the emblem of their greatest victory, and their appointed Professor. "She did not need the lower pleasures; her science was her chief delight." She stood on the platform and taught men, and believed it to be her vocation. Was it not for this that she had toiled during long years of overwork and study, whilst concealing her real purpose under the threadbare cloak of a feigned marriage?

She was a woman of genius with a man's brain, who had come into the world as an example and a leader of all sister brains.

She was, and she was not! Sometimes she felt that she was, and then again she did not. In her latter years she disclaimed the whole of her former life, and silence reigned among the aggrieved sisterhood whenever her name was mentioned; if these latter years had never been, they would have sent the hat round in order to erect a monument in her memory. But that became impossible; silence was best.

She was a woman. She was a woman in spite of all—in spite of a feigned marriage which lasted nearly ten years, in spite of a widowhood which lasted just as long, in spite of her Doctor's degree and the Professorship of Mathematics and the *Prix Bordin*—she was a woman still; not merely a lady, but an unhappy, injured little woman, running through the woods with a wailing cry for her husband.

She was far more of a woman than those luxurious, prattling, sweat-meat-eating young ladies whose languid movements lead us to suppose that they have only just got out of bed; she was more of a woman than the great majority of wives, whose sole occupation it is to increase the world, and to obliterate themselves in so doing.

She, who never charmed any man, was more of a woman than the charmers who turn love into a vocation. She was a new kind of woman, understood by no one, because she was new; she did not even understand herself, and made mistakes for which she was less to blame than the spirit of the age, by whose lash she was driven. And when she became free at last, it was too late to map out a future of her own.

Who knows whether it would have been better for her had she been free from the first? A woman has no destiny of her own; she cannot have one, because she cannot exist alone. Neither can she become a destiny, except indirectly, and through the man. The more womanly she is, and the more richly endowed, all the more surely will her destiny be shaped by the man who takes her to be his wife. If then, even in the case of the average woman, everything depends upon the man whom she marries, how much more true must this be in the case of the woman of genius, in whom not only her womanhood, but also her genius, needs calling to life by the embrace of a man. And if even the average woman cannot attain to the full consciousness of her womanhood without man, how much less can the woman of genius, in whom sex is the actual root of her being, and the source from whence she derives her talent and her *ego*. If her womanhood remains unawakened, then however promising the beginning may be, her life will be nothing more than a gradual decay, and the stronger her vitality, the more terrible will the death-struggle be.

That was Sonia's life. No man took her in his arms and awoke the whole harmony of her being. She became a mother and also a wife, but she never learned what it is to love and be loved again.

5

As I write, the air is filled with a sweet penetrating fragrance, which comes from a tuberose, placed near me on the window-sill. The narrow stalk seems scarcely strong enough to support its thick, knob-like head with the withered buds and sickly, onion-shaped leaves. A tuberose is a poor unshapely thing at the best of times, but this plant is unhealthy because it has lived too long as an ornament in a dark corner of the room under the chandeliers, among albums and photographs. It was dying visibly, decaying at the roots, and there was no help for it. Of course it was a rare flower, but it grew uglier from day to day.

They put it on the window-sill, where there was just room for one plant more, and a pot of mignonette was fetched out of the kitchen garden, attired in an artistic ruffle of green silk paper, and placed under the chandelier in its stead. It fulfilled its duty well, and seemed to thrive admirably among the albums, visiting-cards, and photographs. Nobody looked after the tuberose on the window-sill until it suddenly reminded them of its existence by a strong smell, and even then they only cast a hasty glance and noticed how sickly it looked. When I examined it more closely, I discovered three blossoms in full flower, and quite healthy; the stem was bent forward, and the blossoms were pressing against the window-pane, doing their best to catch the rays of the sun as long as the short autumn day lasted. It thrust forth its dying blossoms and renewed itself now that the great warmer of life was shining on, and embracing it.

To me this flower is an emblem of Sonia Kovalevsky.

She was a rare, strange being in this world of mignonette pots and trivialities. Everything about her was out of proportion, from her thin little body, with its large head, to the sweet fragrance of her genius. She, too, stood in the place of honor under the chandelier, among fashionable poets and thinkers who wrote and thought in accordance with the spirit of the age; and she, too, sickened, as though she desired something better, and the nervous blossoms which her mind thrust forth grew more and more withered, and the thin stem which carried her stretched more and more towards the greater warmer of life, which shines upon and embraces the just and the unjust,—only not her, only not her!

What was the reason? Why did she get none of that love which is rained down upon the most insignificant women in so lavish a manner by impetuous mankind?

"She was not in the least pretty, that is it," reply her several women admirers.

But we women know well that it is not the prettiest women who are the most loved, and that, on the contrary, the most ardent love always falls to the share of those in whom men have something to excuse. Barbey d'Aurevilly, the greatest women's poet, has told us so in his immortal lines.

"She was too old,—that is to say, she aged too early,"—say her women admirers, still anxious to find an explanation.

But that is ridiculous. Sonia Kovalevsky died at the age of forty, and that is the age when a Parisian *grande mondaine* is at the height of her popularity; and as for aging early—! A woman of genius does not grow old as quickly as a teacher in a girl's school, and the fading tuberose which thrusts forth fresh blossoms has a far sweeter and more penetrating fragrance than her white knob-headed sisters.

"She asked too much," asserts Fru Anne Charlotte Edgren-Leffler, Duchess of Cajanello, who was of the same age as Sonia, and married at the time when she died; and her entire book on Sonia is founded on the one argument, that she asked too much of love.

But how is it possible? Does not experience teach us that it is just the women who ask most who receive most? Always make fresh claims,—that is the motto of the majority of ladies in society, and with this solid principle to start from they have none of them failed.

"She had everything that a human being can desire," said that worthy writer, Jonas Lie, in an after-dinner speech. "She had genius, fame, position, liberty, and she took the lead in the education of humanity. But when she had all this it seemed to her as nothing; she stretched out her hand like a little girl, and said, 'Oh, do but give me also this orange.'"

It was kindly said, and also very true. Father Lie was the only person who understood Sonia, and saw that she remained a little girl all her life,—a woman who never reached her maturity. But, tell me, dear Father Lie, do you consider love to be worth no more than an orange?

No, these explanations will never satisfy us; they are far too shallow and simple. The true reason lies deeper; it is more a symptom of the time in which she lived than those who knew her will allow. Even so friendly and intelligent an exponent as Ellen Key, her second biographer, does not seem to be aware of the fact that, although Sonia is a typical woman of her time,—typical of the more earnest upholders of women's rights, and the representative of the highest intellectual accomplishments to which women have attained,—she is also typical of that which the woman of this century loses in the struggle, and of that in which the woman of the future will be the gainer.

If Sonia failed to please,—she whose personal charm was so great, whose vivacity was so prepossessing, as all who knew her declared that it was; if she failed where so many lesser women have succeeded, her failure was entirely due to her ignorance of the art of flirtation,—an art which is as old as sex, and to which men have been accustomed since the world began. Even the most refined, the most highly-developed men, are not geniuses in this matter, where everything has always been most carefully arranged for them. And if they did not fall in love with Sonia, it was due to a kind of purity with which she unconsciously regarded the preliminaries of love,—a kind of nobility which existed in her more modern nature, and a lack of the ancient instinct which had been a lost heritage to her.

Sonia belonged to a class of women who have only been produced in the latter half of our century, but in such large numbers that it is they who have determined the modern type. We cannot help hoping that they are but transitory, so greatly do their assumptions seem opposed to their sex, and yet they are formed of the best material that the age supplies. They are the women who object to begin life by fulfilling their destinies as women, and who consider that they have duties of greater importance than that of becoming wives and mothers; they are the "clever" daughters of the middle-class families, who, as governesses and teachers, swarm in every country in Europe. The popular opinion about them is that they do not want to marry; and as that, by the majority of men, is interpreted to mean that they are no good as wives, they turn to the herd of geese who are driven yearly to the market, and who go cackling to meet their fate. And although the descendants of such fathers and such mothers present a very small amount of intelligence capable of development, yet it is they who form the majority, and the majority is always right. Formerly, it was people's sole object to get their daughters married, clever and stupid alike; it was an understood thing. But nowadays, the ones with "good heads" are set apart to lead celibate lives, while those who are "hard of understanding" are brought into the marriage market. This method of distribution has already become one of the first principles of middle-class economy. The daughters who are considered capable of providing for themselves are given a good education, accompanied by numerous hints as to the large sums which their parents have spent on them; while, together with the inevitable marriage portion, every effort is made to find husbands for the others with as little delay as possible. The first named are "the clever women," but the latter make "the best wives;" and man's sense of justice in the distribution of the good things of this life has fixed a stern practical barrier between these two classes.

The intellectual women themselves were originally to blame for raising a distinction which is so essentially characteristic of our time. They were the first to separate themselves, and to force the narrow-minded *bourgeois* to entertain other than the ordinary ideas concerning women. They thrust aside the dishes which were spread for them on life's table, and grasped at others which had hitherto been considered the sole property of men, such as smoking and drinking. And when it appeared that they were really able to pass examinations and smoke cigarettes, without suffering any apparent harm from either, the spirit of equality, so popular at the present time, was quick to recognize a proof of the equality between man and wife, and to proclaim the equal rights of both, as well as the equality of the brain. They did not mention the other human ingredient, which could never be either equal or identical, because it is always inconvenient to go to the root of a thing, and the arguments of this materialistic century are too superficial ever to go below the surface.

Can it be true that the talented woman has actually forgotten that destiny intended her to be a woman, and bound her by eternal laws? Can it be true that the best women have an unnatural desire to be half men, and that they would prefer to shirk the duties of motherhood? A woman's stupidity would not suffice to account for such an interpretation; it needs all a man's thick-headedness; and yet there is no doubt that that is, to a great extent, the popular view of the case. The women whose intellectual abilities are above the average are often those who lay themselves open to the reproach that they have abandoned their sex; and yet, strange to say, some of them have attained to mature womanhood at an exceedingly early age. Sonia, who was *par préférence* the woman of genius of this century, was only nine years old when she flew into a passion of jealousy, caused by a little girl who was sitting on the knees of her handsome young uncle. She bit him in the arm till it bled, merely because she believed that he liked the child better than herself; that this was something more than mere childish naughtiness, is shown by the fact that her feelings towards her uncle were so changed that from that moment she felt disillusioned, and treated him with coldness.

Disillusioned! Even in their childhood these women have a strong, though indistinct, consciousness of their own worth as compared to ordinary women. They are always on the watch, and they have a good memory. Unlike ordinary young girls, they do not fall in love with mere outward qualities, nor with the first man who happens to cross their path. They wish to marry some one superior to themselves, and they do not mistake a passing passion for love. Then when the first years of adolescence with their hot impulses are past, and a temporary calm sets in, they experience a new desire, which is that they may enter into the full possession of their own being before beginning to raise a new generation. Physical maturity, which has hitherto been considered sufficient, has placed the need for intellectual and psychical maturity in the shade. They want to be grown-up in mind and soul before entering on life; they do not wish to remain children always; they want to develop all their capabilities,—and this longing for individuality, for which the road has not yet been made clear, nearly always leads them astray into the wilderness of study.

This is certainly the case when they are urged on, as Sonia Kovalevsky was, by a remarkable talent. She was not even obliged to follow the usual weary path of study; richly endowed and favorably situated as she was, she discovered a more direct way than is possible to the majority of girl students. Few have been able to begin as she did at the age of seventeen, under the protection of a devoted husband, and under the guidance of learned men, who took a personal interest in her welfare. Few have finished at the age of twenty-four, and have been loaded with distinctions while in the full bloom of their youth, able to stand on the threshold of a rich, full life, while fortune bid them take and choose whatever they might wish.

Yet these were but hollow joys that were offered to her. Those six years of protracted study left her weak in body and soul, and so weary that she needed a long period of idle vegetation, and she felt an aversion from the very studies in which she had accomplished so much. Sonia had overworked herself in the way that most girls overwork themselves in their examinations, whether it be for the university or as teachers; they work on with persistent diligence, looking neither to the right nor to the left, but going straight ahead as though they were the victims of hypnotic suggestion, with all their energies paralyzed except one solitary organ,—the memory. A man never does this; he interrupts his studies with social recreations and by means of a system of hygiene, applied alike to body and soul, from which a woman is excluded, no less on account of her womanly susceptibility than owing to conventional views. During this period of nervous tension, her sex is silent; or if it shows itself at all, it does so only in general irritability.

This was the case with Sonia; but until she became thoroughly engrossed in her work at Weierstrass's, Valdemar Kovalevsky had a great deal to endure. It was not enough for her that she made him run all kinds of messages, which a servant could have done as well, but she was always going to see him in his bachelor apartments, and planning little excursions, and she was never satisfied unless she could have him to herself. Valdemar did not understand her. He had willingly consented to become the husband, in name only, of an undeveloped little girl, and be respected the distorted ideas of the time, which had got firmly fixed into this same little girl's head. It is very natural that Sonia should not have understood the situation; it was not her business to do so, it was his. But she was always irritable and vexed after a *tête-à-tête* of any length with him, and long after his death she used scornfully to say: "He could get on capitally without me. If he had his cigarettes, his cup of tea, and a book, it was all that he required."

Valdemar Kovalevsky, the translator of Brehm's Birds and other popular scientific works into Russian, appears to have belonged to that portion of the male sex who are called "paragons." He drudged diligently, had few wants, always did what was right, and never gave in. But he was in no way suited to Sonia, and the fact of his having agreed to her proposal proves it. After he had gone to Jena to escape from her willful squandering of his time, an estrangement took place between them, and at Berlin she seems to have behaved as though she were ashamed of him. She was living then, as we have seen, with a girl friend who was a fellow-student of hers; and although she let Valdemar fetch her from Weierstrass's, she introduced him to no one, and did not let it appear that he was her husband. Afterwards, when she had finished her studies and undergone a long period of enforced idleness at the time when her nerves were shaken by her father's death, she clung so closely to him that a little warmth came into his stolid nature. But, naturally enough, neither her affection nor the birth of a daughter could change his nature, and even during the short time when they were together at St. Petersburg he allowed an intriguing swindler to come between them. Repulsed, dissatisfied, and saddened, Sonia went to Paris.

She wished to stand alone, and the only way in which this was possible was to turn her studies to account and to work for her own bread. She had given up the wish to be a learned woman; she wanted to be a wife, to be loved and made happy; she had done her best, but it had turned out a failure. It was just about this time that she received an invitation through Professor Mittag-Leffler to be teacher under him in the new high school at Stockholm. He was Fru Leffler's brother, and a pupil of Weierstrass's. Sonia gratefully consented, but a fine ear detects a peculiar undertone in the letters with which she responded.

In Stockholm she did not show the womanly side of her character to any one, least of all to Professor Mittag-Leffler, with whom she was on terms of the most cordial friendship. She found herself in very uncongenial surroundings, in a society where life was conducted on the strictest utilitarian principles. It was the worst time of her life, and one from which her impressionable nature never entirely recovered.

Before this, however, while she was in Paris, she had an experience which was truly characteristic of her.

In the interval which elapsed between her separation from her husband and his death, she made the acquaintance of a young Pole, who was, as Fru Leffler tells us, "a revolutionary, a mathematician, a poet, with a soul aglow with enthusiasm like her own. It was the first time that she had met any one who really understood her, who shared her varying moods, and sympathized with all her thoughts and dreams as he did. They were nearly always together, and the short hours when they were apart were spent in writing long effusions to each other. They were wild about the idea that human beings were created in couples, and that men and women are only half beings until they have found their other half...." He was with her by night and day, for he could seldom make up his mind to go before two o'clock in the morning, when he would climb over the garden wall, quite regardless of what people would think. Fru Leffler, who had passed the twenty years of her first marriage in the outer courts of the temple of Hymen, and only learned to know love and the joys of motherhood at the age of forty, alludes to this incident as being "very curious." Because the two did nothing but talk, talk, talk, reveling in each other's conversation, and assuring one another that they "could never be united," because "he was going to keep himself pure" for the girl who was wandering about on this or another planet, and keeping herself for him.

One would imagine that this was childish nonsense, and that a woman of Sonia's intelligence, with her position in the world, must surely have sent the silly boy about his business as soon as he began to talk in this strain. But no! her soul melted into his "like two flames which unite in one common glow." And there they sat, nervous and excited, unable to tear themselves away from each other, flinging endless chains of words backwards and forwards across the table, and pouring streams of witticism into Danaïde's barrel, talking as though life depended upon it, for there must not be any pauses,—anything was better than those dreadful pauses, when one seems to hear nothing but the beating of one's own pulse, when shy eyes meet another's, and cold damp hands seek for a corner in which to hide themselves.

We do not know what pleasure the "pure" young mathematician, poet, and Pole could find in this, nor do we care; we leave that to those who take an interest in the ebullitions of model young men of his class. The only part of the situation with which we are concerned is Sonia herself, and she is extremely interesting. In the first place, such a situation as this is never brought about by the man, or, at any rate, not more than once; and a woman cannot be entrapped into it against her will. The silliest schoolgirl knows how to get rid of a troublesome man when she wishes; they all do it brilliantly. It is quite a different matter when she wants him to stay, when she is trembling with excitement, and dreads the moment when he will rise to go. Who is not well acquainted with the situation, especially when the parties concerned are an intelligent girl and a dilettante man? In this case Sonia was the intelligent girl. Her behavior was that of a young lady who is painfully conscious of her own inexperience. A married woman who knows what love is can be calm in the presence of the warmest passion. She knows so well the path which leads astray that she no longer fears the unknown, and uncertainty has no attraction for her.

I shall probably be told that it is the married women who enjoy these situations most. That is quite true. There are many married women for whom marriage is neither *l'amour goût*, nor *l'amour passion*, nor *l'amour savant*, nor yet any other love, but a mere mechanical trans-action. If the husband is indifferent he cannot rouse his wife's love. Not motherhood, but the lover's kiss, awakes the Sleeping Beauty. And in the Madonna's immaculate conception the Church has incarnated the virgin mother in a profound symbol, which only needs a psychological interpretation to make it applicable to thousands of every-day cases.

Extraordinary though it may seem, Sonia was on this occasion, as on many other occasions in later life, a woman who experienced desire without being in the least aware of it. She was like a virgin mother who had borne a child without knowing man's love. Valdemar Kovalevsky, who seems to me to have been incapable of filling any position in life, was certainly not the husband for Sonia, who, as a woman of genius, cannot be judged by the same standard as ordinary women. The average man is certainly not suited to be the husband of an exceptional woman with an original mind and sensitive temperament. But they do not know themselves; for it is in the nature of great talents to remain hidden from their owners, who have a long way to go before they attain to the full realization of their own powers. Only those geniuses whose talents have little or no connection with their individuality are sufficiently alive to their own claims not to fall short in life, and not to allow themselves to be hindered by any natural modesty.

Modesty comes only too naturally to great geniuses. They are conscious of being different from other people, yet when they are com-pelled to come forward they only do so under protest, and then beg every one's pardon. The richest natures are the least conscious of their own powers; they are ashamed because they think that they are offering a copper, when in reality they are giving away kingdoms. This is doubly true of the woman who knows nothing of her own powers until the man comes to reveal them to her.

It was the same with Sonia. She was always giving away hand-fuls,—her mind, her learning, her social gifts; she placed them all at the disposal of others; yet when she, who felt the eternal loneliness which accompanies genius, asked for the entire affection of another, she was told that she asked too much. There can be no agreement between that which genius has the right to ask, and mediocrity the power to give. It was not a very strong affection that she had for the young Pole, and, such as it was, it did but intensify her sense of loneliness. It was at Paris that she received the news of her husband's suicide; and she, who suffered so acutely from every successive death in her family, seemed doomed to receive one blow after another at the hand of fate. She had scarcely recovered from a nervous fever, resulting from the shock, when she was called to Stockholm by the supporters of women's rights,—to Stockholm, where her soul congealed, her mind was unsatisfied, and where her body was to die.

6

I shall only give a hasty sketch of the years that followed. Fru Leffler has given us a detailed account of them in her book on Sonia, and Ellen Key, in her life of Fru Leffler, has made the crooked straight, and has filled in some of the gaps. I shall merely touch upon this period for the sake of those of my readers who are not acquainted with either of the above-mentioned works. These years were about the most lifeless, and, psychologically speaking, the most empty in Sonia's life. She was called upon to take part in a movement which from its commencement was doomed to fail on account of its narrow principles. The social circle was divided into two separate groups, one of which consisted of ladies and dilettante youths, very excitable and full of zeal for reform, but without a single really superior man among them; the other was of an essentially Swedish character, consisting chiefly of men; the "better class" of women were excluded, and drinking bouts, night reveling, club life, song-singing, and easy-going friendship was the rule. These included a few talented people among their number, and expressed the utmost contempt for the other group. For the first time in her life Sonia was made to do ordinary every-day work, and to exert herself after the manner of a mere drudge, or a cart-horse, for payment.

Her position rendered her dependent on the moral standard of a *clique*. With the flexibility of her Russian nature, she renounced the freedom to which she had been accustomed, and devoted herself to her duties as lecturer under a professor. This work soon began to weary her to death. Mathematics lost their charm now that the genius of old Weierstrass was no longer there to elucidate the problems, and to encourage her to do that which women had hitherto been unable to accomplish.

For some time she struggled on through thick and thin, without however sinking low enough to give her superiors no longer any cause to shake their heads or to admonish her. Lively, witty, and unassuming, the task of entertaining people at their social gatherings fell to her share, and she bore the weight of it without a murmur, until her wasted amiability resulted in an undue familiarity in the circle of her admirers, of both sexes, causing her much vexation. When the first excitement of novelty was passed, she devoted herself chiefly to her true but stolid friend, Anne Charlotte Leffler. It was one of those friendships which are getting to be very common now that women are becoming intellectual; it was not the result of any deep mutual sympathy, nor was it formed out of the fulness of their lives, but rather from the consciousness that there was something lacking, as when two *minus* combine in the attempt to form one *plus*. Then as soon as the *plus* is there, all interest in one another, and all mutual sympathy is a thing of the past, as it proved in this case, when the Duke of Cajanello appeared on Fru Leffler's horizon, and she afterwards, in the honeymoon of her happiness, possibly with the best of intentions, but with very little tact or sympathy, wrote her obituary book on Sonia.

One of the results of this friendship was a series of unsuccessful literary attempts, for which the material was provided by Sonia, and dramatized by Fru Leffler. The latter tried to put Sonia's psychological, intuitive experiences into a realistic shape, and the result was, as might be expected, a failure. Sonia was a mystic, whose whole being was one indistinct longing without beginning and without end; Fru Leffler was an enlightened woman, daughter of a college rector, "who worked incessantly at her own development." Even while the work of collaboration was in progress, a slight friction began to make itself felt between the two friends. Fru Leffler was vexed at having, as she expressed it, "repudiated her own child" in the story called "Round about Marriage," in which she attempted to describe the lives of women who remain unmarried.

The storms raised by Sonia's vivid imagination oppressed her, and imported a foreign element into her sober style, resulting in long padded novels, which were too ambitious, and had a false ring about them. Her influence on Sonia produced the opposite result. Sonia saw that Fru Leffler was less talented than she had supposed, and this made her place greater confidence in her own merits as an author. She began to write a story of her own youth, called "The Sisters Rajevsky," which we have already mentioned, followed by a story about the so-called Nihilists, "Vera Barantzova;" both these books displayed a wider experience, and contained the promise of greater things than any of the contemporaneous literature by women, but they did not receive the recognition which they deserved, because nobody understood the characters which she depicted.

Up till now there has been a fundamental error in all the attempts made to understand Sonia Kovalevsky, and the fault is chiefly due to Fru Leffler, who wrote of her from the following standpoint:—

"I am great and you are great,
We are both equally great."

Sonia and her biographer are by no means "equally great." To
compare Fru Leffler to Sonia is like comparing a nine days' wonder to
an eternal phenomenon. One is an ordinary woman with a carefully
cultivated talent, while the other is one of those mysteries who, from
time to time, make their appearance in the world, in whom nature
seems to have overstepped her boundaries, and who are created to live
lonely lives, to suffer and to die without having ever attained the full
possession of their own being.

In the year 1888, at the age of thirty-eight, Sonia learned for the first
time to know the love which is a woman's destiny. M. K. was a great,
heavy Russian boyar, who had been a professor, but was dismissed on
account of his free-thinking views. He was a dissipated man and rich,
and had spent his time in travelling since he left Russia. He was no
longer young, like the Duke of Cajanello. A few years older than Sonia,
he was one of those complacent, self-centered characters who have
never known what it is to long for sympathy, who are totally devoid of
ideals, and are not given to vain illusions. Comparatively speaking, an
older woman always has a better chance with a man younger than herself, and there was nothing very surprising in the love which the young
and insignificant Duke bestowed on Fru Leffler. With Sonia it was quite
different. The boyar had already enjoyed as many of the good things of
this world as he desired; he was both practical and skeptical, the kind
of man whom women think attractive, and who boast that they understand women. I am not at liberty to mention his name, as he is still alive
and enjoys good health. He was interested in Sonia, as much as he was
capable of being interested in any one, because she was a compatriot to
be proud of, and he also liked her because she was good company, but
Sonia never acquired all the power over him which she should have had.
He was not like a susceptible young man who is influenced by the first

woman who has really given him the full passion of her love. The long-repressed love which was now lavished upon him by the woman who was no longer young had none of the surprise of novelty in it, not even the unexpected treasure of flattered vanity. He accepted it calmly, and never for a moment did he allow it to interfere with his mode of life. Even though he had no wife, his bachelor's existence had never lacked the companionship of women. Sonia should occupy the position of wife, but an ardent lover it was no longer in his power to be.

The conflict points plainly to a double rupture between them,—the one internal and the other external,—both brought about by the spirit of the age.

Sonia's womanhood had awakened in her the first time they met, and he became her first love. She loved him as a young girl loves, with a trembling and ungovernable joy at finding all that had hitherto been hidden in herself; she rejoiced in the knowledge that he was there, that she would see him again to-morrow as she had seen him to-day, that she could touch him, hold him with her hands. She lived only when she saw him; her senses were dulled when he was no longer there. It was then that Stockholm became thoroughly hateful to her; it seemed to hold her fast in its clutches, to crush the woman in her, and to deprive her of her nationality. He represented the South,—the great world of intellect and freedom; but above all else, he was home, he was Russia! He was the emblem of her native land; he had come speaking the language in which her nurse had sung to her, in which her father and sister and all the loved and lost had spoken to her; he was her hearth and home in the dreary world. But more than all this, he was the only man capable of arousing her love.

But if she took a short holiday and followed him to Paris and Italy, his cold greeting was sure to chill her inmost being, and instead of the comfort which she had hoped to find in his love and sympathy, she was thrown back upon herself, more miserable and disappointed than before.

Her spirits were beginning to give way. It seemed as though the world were growing empty around her and the darkness deepening, while she stood in the midst of it all, alone and unprotected. But what drove matters to a climax was that their most intimate daily intercourse took place just at the time when she was in Paris working hard, and sitting up at nights. When she was awarded the *Prix Bordin* on Christmas Eve, 1888, in the presence of the greatest French mathematicians, she forgot that she was a European celebrity, whose name would endure forever and be numbered among the women who had outstripped all others; she was only conscious of being an overworked woman, suffering from one of those nervous illnesses when white seems turned to black, joy to sorrow,—enduring the unutterable misery caused by mental and physical exhaustion, when the night brings no rest to the tortured nerves. As is always the case with productive natures under like circumstances, her passions were at their highest pitch, and she needed sympathy from without to give relief. It was then that she received an offer of marriage from the man whom she loved; but she was too well aware of the gulf which lay between his gentlemanly bearing and her devouring passion to accept it, and determined that since she could not have all she would have nothing. It may be that she was haunted by the recollection of her first marriage, or she may have been influenced by the woman's rights standpoint which weighs as in a scale: For so and so many ounces of love, I must have so and so many ounces of love and fidelity; and for so and so many yards of virtuous behavior, I have a right to expect exactly the same amount from him.

It happened, however, that the man in question would not admit of such calculations, and Sonia went back to Stockholm and her hated university work with the painful knowledge of "never having been all in all to anybody." After a time she began to realize that love is not a thing which can be weighed and measured. She now concentrated her strength in an attempt to free herself from her work at Stockholm, which had been turned into a life-long appointment since she won the *Prix Bordin*; she longed to get away from Sweden, where she felt very lonely, having no one to whom she could confide her thoughts. She had some hopes of being given an honorary appointment as a member of the Imperial Russian Academy, which would place her in a position of pecuniary independence, with the liberty to reside where she pleased. But when she returned to her work at Stockholm in the beginning of the year 1891, after a trip to Italy in company with the man whom she loved, it was with the conviction, grown stronger than ever, of not being able to put up with the loneliness and emptiness of her existence any longer, and with the determination of throwing everything aside and accepting his proposal.

She came to this decision while suffering from extreme weariness. Her Russian temperament was very much opposed to the manner of her life for the last few years. Her spirits, which wavered between a state of exaltation and apathy, were depressed by a regular routine of work and social intercourse, and she was never allowed the thorough rest which she so greatly needed. In one year she lost all who were dear to her; and though dissatisfied with her own life, she was able to sympathize deeply with her beloved sister Anjuta, whose proud dreams of youth were either doomed to destruction, or else their fulfilment was accompanied with disappointment, while she herself was dying slowly, body and soul. Life had dealt hardly with both these sisters. When Sonia travelled home for the last time, after exchanging the warm, cheerful South for the cold, dismal North, she broke down altogether. Alone and over-tired as she always was on these innumerable journeys, which were only undertaken in order to cure her nervous restlessness, her spirits were no longer able to encounter the discomforts of travel, and she gave way. The perpetual changes, whether in rain, wind, or snow, accompanied by all the small annoyances, such as getting money changed, and finding no porters, overpowered her, and for a short time life seemed to have lost all its value. With an utter disregard for consequences, she exposed herself to all winds and weathers, and arrived ill at Stockholm, where her course of lectures was to begin immediately. A heavy cold ensued, accompanied by an attack of fever; and so great was her longing for fresh air, that she ran out into the street on a raw February day in a light dress and thin shoes.

Her illness was short; she died a couple of days after it began. Two friends watched beside her, and she thanked them warmly for the care they took of her,—thanked them as only strangers are thanked. They had gone home to rest before the death-struggle began, and there was no one with her but a strange nurse, who had just arrived. She died alone, as she had lived,—died, and was buried in the land where she had not wished to live, and where her best strength had been spent.

7

There is yet another picture behind the one depicted in these pages. It is large, dark, and mysterious, like a reflection in the water; we see it, but it melts away each time we try to grasp it.

When we know the story of a person's life, and are acquainted with their surroundings and the conditions under which they have been brought up; when we have been told about their sufferings, and the illness of which they died, we imagine that we know all about them, and are able to form a more or less correct portrait of them in our mind's eye, and we even think that we are in a position to judge of their life and character. There is scarcely any one whose life is less veiled to the public gaze than Sonia Kovalevsky's. She was very frank and communicative, and took quite a psychological interest in her own character; she had nothing to conceal, and was known by a large number of people throughout Europe. She lived her life before the eyes of the public, and died of inflammation of the lungs, brought on by an attack of influenza.

Such was Sonia Kovalevsky's life as depicted by Fru Leffler, in a manner which reveals a very limited comprehension of her subject; the chief thing missing is the likeness to Sonia.

This sketch was afterwards corrected and completed with great sympathy and delicacy by Ellen Key, but she has also failed to catch the likeness of Sonia Kovalevsky.

And mine—written as it is with the full consciousness of being better able to understand her than either of these two, partly on account of the impressions left by my own half-Russian childhood; partly, too, because in some ways my temperament resembles hers—my sketch, although it is an analysis of her life, is not Sonia Kovalevsky.

She is still standing there, supernaturally great, like a shadow when the moon rises, which seems to grow larger the longer one looks at it; and as I write this, I feel as though she were as near to me as a body that one knocks up against in the dark. She comes and goes. Sometimes she appears close beside me sitting on the flower-table, a little bird-like figure, and I seem to see her quite distinctly; then, as soon as I begin to realize her presence, she has gone. And I ask myself,—Who is she? I do not know; she did not know it herself. She lived, it is true, but she never lived her own, real, individual life.

She remains there still,—a form which came out of the darkness and went back into the same. She was a thorough child of the age in every little characteristic of her aimless life; she was a woman of this century, or rather, she was what this century forces a woman to be,—a genius for nothing, a woman for nothing, ever struggling along a road which leads to nowhere, and fainting on the way as she strives to attain a distant mirage. Tired to death, and yet afraid to die, she died because the instinct for self-preservation forsook her for the space of a single instant; died only to be buried under a pile of obituary notices, and forgotten for the next novelty. But behind them all she stands, an immortal personality, hot and volcanic as the world's center, a thorough woman, yet more than a woman. Her brain rose superior to sex, and learned to think independently, only to be dragged down again and made subservient to sex; her soul was full of mysticism, conscious of the Infinite existing in her little body, and out of her little body again soaring up towards the Infinite,—a one day's superficial consciousness which allowed itself to be led astray by public opinion, yet possessing, all the while, a sub-consciousness, which, poetically viewed, clung fast to the eternal realities in her womanly frame, and would not let them rise to the brain, which, freed from the body, floated in empty space. Hers was a queenly mind, feeding a hundred beggars at her board,—giving to all, but confiding in none.

Ellen Key once said to me: "When she shook hands, you felt as if a little bird with a beating heart had fluttered into your hand and out again." And another friend, Hilma Strandberg, a young writer of great promise, whose after career belied its commencement, said, after her first meeting with Sonia, that she had felt as though the latter's glance had pierced her through and through, after which she seemed to be dissecting her soul, bit by bit, every bit vanishing into thin air; this psychical experience was followed by such violent bodily discomfort that she almost fainted, and it was only with the greatest difficulty that she managed to get home.

Both these descriptions prove that Sonia's hands and eyes were the most striking part of her personality. Many anecdotes are told about her penetrating glance, but this is the only one which mentions her hands, although it is true that Fru Leffler remarked that they were very much disfigured by veins. But this one is sufficient to complete a picture of her which I remember to have seen: she has a slender little child's body, and her hands are the hands of a child, with nervous, crooked little fingers, anxiously bent inwards; and in one hand she clasps a book, with such visible effort that it makes one's heart ache to look at her.

The hands often afford better material for psychological study than the face, and they give a deeper and more truthful insight into the character because they are less under control. There are people with fine, clever faces, whose hands are like sausages,—fleshy and veinless, with thick stumpy fingers which warn us to beware of the animated mask. And there are round, warm, sensuous faces, with full, almost thick lips, which are obviously contradicted by pale, blue-veined, sickly-looking hands. The momentary amount of intellectual power which a person has at his disposal can change the face, but the hands are of a more physical nature, and their speech is a more physical one. Sonia's face was lit up by the soul in her eyes, which bore witness to the intense interest which she took in everything that was going on around her; but the weak, nervous, trembling little hands told of the unsatisfied, helpless child, who was never to attain the full development of her womanhood.

Neurotic Keynotes

1

Last year there was a book published in London with the extraordinary title of "Keynotes." Three thousand copies were sold in the course of a few months, and the unknown author became a celebrity. Soon afterwards the portrait of a lady appeared in "The Sketch." She had a small, delicate face, with a pained and rather tired expression, and a curious, questioning look in the eyes; it was an attractive face, very gentle and womanly, and yet there was something disillusioned and unsatisfied about it. This lady wrote under the pseudonym of George Egerton, and "Keynotes" was her first book.

It was a strange book! too good a book to become famous all at once. It burst upon the world like the opening buds in spring, like the cherry blossom after the first cold shower of rain. What can have made this book so popular in the England of to-day, which is as totally devoid of all true literature as Germany itself? Was it only the writer's strong individuality, which each successive page impressed upon the reader's nerves more vividly and more painfully than the last? The reader, did I say? Yes, but not the male reader. There are very few men who have a sufficiently keen appreciation for a woman's feelings to be able to put their own minds and souls into the swing of her confession, and to accord it their full sympathy. Yet there are such men. We may perhaps come across two or three of them in a lifetime, but they disappear from our sight, as we do from theirs. And they are not readers. Their sympathy is of a deeper, more personal character, and as far as the success of a book is concerned, it need not be taken into consideration at all.

"Keynotes" is not addressed to men, and it will not please them. It is not written in the style adopted by the other women Georges,—George Sand and George Eliot,—who wrote from a man's point of view, with the solemnity of a clergyman or the libertinism of a drawing-room hero. There is nothing of the man in this book, and no attempt is made to imitate him, even in the style, which springs backwards and forwards as restlessly as a nervous little woman at her toilet, when her hair will not curl and her stay-lace breaks. Neither is it a book which favors men; it is a book written against them, a book for our private use.

There have been such books before; old-maid literature is a lucrative branch of industry, both in England and Germany (the two most unliterary countries in Europe), and that is probably the reason why the majority of authoresses write as though they were old maids. But there are no signs of girlish prudery in "Keynotes;" it is a liberal book, indiscreet in respect of the intimacies of married life, and entirely without respect for the husband; it is a book with claws and teeth ready to scratch and bite when the occasion offers,—not the book of a woman who married for the sake of a livelihood, but the book of a devoted wife, who would be inseparable from her husband if only he were not so tiresome, and dull, and stupid, such a thorough man, insufferable at times, and yet indispensable as the husband always is to the wife.

And it is the book of a gentlewoman!

We have had tell-tale women before, but Heaven preserve us! Fru Skram is a man in petticoats; she speaks her mind plainly enough,—rather too plainly to suit my taste. "Gyp," a distinguished Frenchwoman, has written "Autour du Mariage," and she cannot be said to mince matters either. But here we have something quite different; something which does not in the least resemble Gyp's frivolous worldliness or Amalie Skram's coarseness. Mrs. Egerton would shudder at the thought of washing dirty linen in public, and she could not, even if she were to force herself, treat the relationship between husband and wife with cynical irony, and she does not force herself in the very least.

She writes as she really is, because she cannot do otherwise. She has had an excellent education, and is a lady with refined tastes, with something of that innocence of the grown woman which is almost more touching than a girl's innocence, because it proves how little of his knowledge of life in general, and his sex in particular, the Teutonic husband confides to his wife. She stands watching him,—an eating, loving, smoking organism. Heavens! how wearisome! So loved, and yet so wearisome! It is unbearable! And she retreats into herself, and realizes that she is a woman.

It is almost universal amongst women, especially Germans, that they do not take man as seriously as he likes to imagine. They think him comical,—not only when they are married to him, but even before that, when they are in love with him. Men have no idea what a comical appearance they present, not only as individuals, but as a race. The comic part about a man is that he is so different from women, and that is just what he is proudest of. The more refined and fragile a woman is, the more ridiculous she is likely to find the clumsy great creature who takes such a roundabout way to gain his comical ends.

To young girls especially man offers a perpetual excuse for a laugh, and a secret shudder. When men find a group of women laughing among themselves, they never suspect that it is they who are the cause of it. And that again is so comic! The better a man is, the more he is in earnest when he makes his pathetic appeal for a great love; and woman, who takes a special delight in playing a little false, even when there is no necessity, becomes as earnest and solemn as he, when all the time she is only making fun of him. A woman wants amusement, wants change; a monotonous existence drives her to despair, whereas a man thrives on monotony, and the cleverer he is the more he wishes to retire into himself, that he may draw upon his own resources; a clever woman needs variety, that she may take her impressions from without.

... The early blossoms of the cherry-tree shudder beneath the cold rain which has burst their scales; this shudder is the deepest vibration in Mrs. Egerton's book. What is the subject? A little woman in every imaginable mood, who is placed in all kinds of likely and unlikely circumstances: in every story it is the same little woman with a difference, the same little woman, who is always loved by a big, clumsy, comic man, who is now good and well-behaved, now wild, drunk, and brutal; who sometimes ill-treats her, sometimes fondles her, but never understands what it is that he ill-treats and fondles. And she sits like a true Englishwoman with her fishing-rod, and while she is waiting for a bite, "her thoughts go to other women she has known, women good and bad, school friends, casual acquaintances, women-workers,—joyless machines for grinding daily corn, unwilling maids grown old in the endeavor to get settled, patient wives who bear little ones to indifferent husbands until they wear out,—a long array. She busies herself with questioning. Have they, too, this thirst for excitement, for change, this restless craving for sun and love and motion? Stray words, half confidences, glimpses through soul-chinks of suppressed fires, actual outbreaks, domestic catastrophes,—how the ghosts dance in the cells of her memory! And she laughs—laughs softly to herself because the denseness of man, his chivalrous conservative devotion to the female idea he has created, blinds him, perhaps happily, to the problems of her complex nature, ... and well it is that the workings of our hearts are closed to them, that we are cunning enough or *great* enough to seem to be what they would have us, rather than be what we are. But few of them have had the insight to find out the key to our seeming contradictions,—the why a refined, physically fragile woman will mate with a brute, a mere male animal with primitive passions, and love him; the why strength and beauty appeal more often than the more subtly fine qualities of mind or heart; the why women (and not the innocent ones) will condone sins that men find hard to forgive in their fellows. They have all overlooked the eternal wildness, the untamed primitive savage temperament that lurks in the mildest, best woman. Deep in through ages of convention this primeval trait burns, an untamable quantity that may be concealed, but is never eradicated by culture,—the keynote of woman's witchcraft and woman's strength."

They are not stories which Mrs. Egerton tells us. She does not care for telling stories. They are keynotes which she strikes, and these keynotes met with an extraordinary and most unexpected response. They struck a sympathetic chord in women, which found expression in a multitude of letters, and also in the sale of the book. An author can hope for no happier fate than to receive letters which re-echo the tune that he has discovered in his own soul. Those who have received them know what pleasant feelings they call forth. We often do not know where they come from, we cannot answer them, nor should we wish to do so if we could. They give us a sudden insight into the hidden center of a living soul, where we can gaze into the secret, yearning life, which is never lived in the sight of the world, but is generally the best part of a person's nature; we feel the sympathetic clasp of a friendly hand, and our own soul is filled with a thankfulness which will never find expression in words. The dark world seems filled with unknown friends, who surround us on every side like bright stars in the night.

Mrs. Egerton had struck the fundamental chord in woman's nature, and her book was received with applause by hundreds of women. The critic said: "The woman in 'Keynotes' is an exceptional type, and we can only deal with her as such." "Good heavens! How stupid they are!" laughed Mrs. Egerton. Numberless women wrote to her, women whom she did not know, and whose acquaintance she never made. "We are quite ordinary, every-day sort of people," they said; "we lead trivial, unimportant lives; but there is something in us which vibrates to your touch, for we, too, are such as you describe." "Keynotes" took like wildfire.

There is nothing tangible in the book to which it can be said to owe its significance. Notes are not tangible. The point on which it differs from all other well-known books by women is the intensity of its awakened consciousness as woman. It follows no pattern and is quite independent of any previous work; it is simply full of a woman's individuality. It is not written on a large scale, and it does not reveal a very expansive temperament. But, such as it is, it possesses an amount of nervous energy which carries us along with it, and we must read every page carefully until the last one is turned, not peep at the end to see what is going to happen, as we do when reading a story with a plot; we must read every page for its own sake, if we would feel the power of its different moods, varying from feverish haste to wearied rest.

2

Nearly a year afterwards, a book was published in Paris by Lemerre, called "Dilettantes." Instead of the author's name there were three stars, but a catalogue issued by a less illustrious publisher is not so discreet. It mentions the bearer of a well-known pseudonym as the author of the book; a lady who first gained a reputation by translating Hungarian folk songs into French, for which she received an acknowledgment from the *Académie Française*, and who afterwards introduced Scandinavian authors to Paris, thereby deserving the thanks of both countries. She has also made herself a name in literary circles by her original and clever criticisms. Those who are behind the scenes know that the translator's pseudonym and the three stars conceal a lady who belongs to the highest aristocracy of Austria, and who is herself a "dilettante," inasmuch as she writes without any pecuniary object, and that, quite independent of her public, she writes and translates what she pleases. Her social position has placed her among intellectual people; on her mother's side she is descended from one of the foremost families among the Austrian nobility, and she has lived in Paris from her childhood, where she has enjoyed the society of the best authors, and acquired a French style which, for richness, beauty, and grace, might well cause many an older French author to envy her. It is in this French, which she finds more pliable than the homely Viennese German, that this curious book is written.

I search high and low for words in which to describe the nature of this book, but in vain. It is womanly to such an extent, and in such a peculiar way, that we lack the words to express it in a language which has not yet learned to distinguish between the art of man and the art of woman in the sphere of production. It has the same effect upon us as Mrs. Egerton's "Keynotes."

The same reason which makes it difficult to understand this Celtic woman with the English pseudonym, makes it equally difficult to draw an intelligible picture of this French-writing Austrian, with the Polish and Hungarian blood mingled in her veins. But it is not the cross between the races, nor, we might add, is it any cross between soul and ideas which makes these two women so incomprehensible and almost enigmatical; one is twice married, the other a girl, although she is perhaps the more wearied and disillusioned of the two,—and yet it is not the outer circumstances of their lives which render both what they are, it is something in themselves, quite apart from the experience which beautifies and develops a woman's character; it is the keynote of their being which retreats shyly to the background as though afraid of the public gaze. It is the beginning of a series of personal confessions at first hand, and forms an entirely new department in women's literature. Hitherto, as I have already said, all books, even the best ones, written by women, are imitations of men's books, with the addition of a single high-pitched, feminine note, and are therefore nothing better than communications received at second hand. But at last the time has come when woman is so keenly alive to her own nature that she reveals it when she speaks, even though it be in riddles.

I have often pointed out that men only know the side of our character which they wish to see, or which it may please us to show them. If they are thorough men, they seek the woman in us, because they need it as the complement to their own nature; but often they seek our "soul," our "mind," our "character," or whatever else they may happen to look upon as the beautifying veil of our existence. Something may come of the first, but of the last nothing. Mrs. Egerton interpreted man from the first of the above standpoints; she wrote of him, half in hate and half in admiration; her men are great clowns. The author of "Dilettantes" wrote from the opposite point of view; her man is the smooth-speaking *poseur*, of whom she writes with a shrug of the shoulders and an expression of mild contempt.

Both feel themselves to be so utterly different from what they were told they were, and which men believe them to be. They do not understand it at all; they do not understand themselves in the very least. They interpret nothing with the understanding, but their instinct makes them feel quite at home with themselves and leads them to assert their own natures. They are no longer a reflection which man molds into an empty form; they are not like Galatea, who became a living woman through Pygmalion's kiss; they were women before they knew Pygmalion,—such thorough women that Pygmalion is often no Pygmalion to them at all, but a stupid lout instead.

It is a fearful disappointment, and causes a woman—and many a womanly woman too—to shrink from man and scan him critically. "You?" she cries. "No, it were better not to love at all!" But the day is coming—

And when the day has come, then woman will be as bad as Strindberg's Megoras, or as humorous as a certain poetess who sent a portrait of her husband to a friend, with this inscription: "My old Adam;" or else she may meet with the same fate as Countess Resa in the anonymous book of a certain well-known authoress. She will commit suicide in one way or the other. She will not kill herself like Countess Resa, but she will kill a part of her nature. And these women, who are partly dead, carry about a corpse in their souls from whence streams forth an odor as of death; these women, whose dead natures have the power of charming men with a mystery they would gladly solve,—these women are our mothers, sisters, friends, teachers, and we scarcely know the meaning of the shiver down our backs which we feel in their presence. A very keen consciousness is needed to dive down deep enough in ourselves to dis-cover the reason, and very subtle, spiritual tools are necessary to grasp the process and to reproduce it. The Austrian authoress possessed both these requisites. But there is also a third which is equally indispensable to any one who would draw such a portrait of themselves, and that is the distinguished manner of a noble and self-confident nature, in which everything can be said.

She has something besides, which gives the book a special attraction of its own, and that is her extremely modern, artistic feeling, which teaches how the laws of painting can be brought to bear upon the art of writing, and gives her a keen appreciation of the value of sound in relation to language.

There is a picture by Claude Monet,—pale, golden sunshine upon a misty sea. There is scarcely anything to be seen beyond this faint golden haze, resting upon the shimmering, transparent water, painted in rain-bow colors, pale as opal. There is just a faint suggestion of a prom-ontory, rising up from the warm, southern sea, and something which looks like a squadron of fishing boats in the far distance. It is not quite day, but it is already light,—one of those cool mornings which precede a dazzling day. It is years since last I saw this picture, but it charmed me so much that I have never forgotten it. It is in consequence of this same sense for fine shades of color, applied in this instance to the soul, that "Dilettantes" was written.

It is a very quiet book, and just as there is not a single strong color in Monet's picture, so there is not a single high note in this book. We feel like gazing down into the water which glides and glides along, carrying with it seaweed, dead bodies, and men, but always in silence,—a most uneventful book. But beneath this almost lethargical stillness is enacted a tragedy in which a life is at stake, and the stake is lost, and death is the consequence. The deadliest blow against another's soul is caused, not by words, but by deafness and indifference, by neglect at the moment when the heart yearns for love, and the bud is ready to blossom into flower beneath a single breath of sympathy. Next morning, when you go to look at it, you find it withered; it is then too late for your warm breath and willing fingers to force it open; you only make it worse, and at last the buds fall to the ground.

The famous unknown has called her book "Dilettantes," although there is but one lady in it to whom the name applies. Can it be that, by her use of the plural, she meant to include herself with the heroine? The supposition seems not unlikely.

She introduces us to a colony of artists in Paris, amongst whom is Baron Mark Sebenyi, an Hungarian magnate, who is a literary dilettante. At the house of the old Princess Ebendorf he makes the acquaintance of her niece, Theresia Thaszary, and feels himself drawn towards her as his "twin soul." During the Princess's long illness, they become engaged, and when the Princess dies he continues his visits to the Countess as though her aunt were still alive, and he spends his hours of literary work in her house, because, as he says, her presence is an indispensable source of inspiration to him. Countess Resa is one of those whom a life of constant travel has rendered cosmopolitan. Her life is passed in a state of mental torpor which is more general, and, I should like to add, more normal, among young girls than men imagine or married women remember; she was neither contented nor discontented while she lived with her aunt, and she continues the same now, with Mark continually beside her. She is glad to have him with her; she feels a certain attraction in his manly and sympathetic presence, and his behavior towards herself is so decorous that it seldom happens that so much as a pressure of the hand passes between them. She knows that Mark has relations with other women, but that fact does not enter into her womanly consciousness at all.

All goes well until a fashionable friend of hers, a rather vulgar lady, asks her when she means to marry Mark, and persuades her to go into society, although she has no desire to do so, and is perfectly content with the sameness of her life. In society she finds that her friendship with Mark attracts observation, and this is the first shock which leads to an awakening. In the long winter hours, while she is sitting still in the room where he is writing, she suddenly realizes the situation, and feels that it is like a lover's *tête-à-tête*. His behavior in society irritates her in a hundred little ways, because she knows that he is not true to his real nature, and that he gives way to his vanity as an author and poses in public. Mark has no intention of marrying her; he is quite content with matters as they stand. Cold-hearted, and probably aged before his time, he feels drawn towards her by a kind of distant, erotic feeling, and he seeks her society for the sake of the drawing-room where he can make himself thoroughly at home and bring his artist friends; he likes her because he is not bound to her, and he has never tired of her because she was never his.

Spring comes. They make expeditions round about Paris, and are constantly together; she is in a state of nervous excitement, and the more she feels drawn towards him the more she tries to avoid him. There are moments when he too feels his hand tremble, if by chance it comes into contact with hers. Their friendship with one another has become a hindrance to any greater friendship between them; and he is too much taken up with himself, too accustomed to have her always busily attending to him, to notice the change which is gradually taking place in her. Her love dwindles beneath the cold influence of doubt, which increases the more as she feels herself rejected by the man she loves. Ignorant though she be, she is possessed of an intuitive knowledge which is the heritage of many generations of culture, which enables her to read him through and through, until she conceives an antipathy for him,—the man whose love she desires,—an antipathy which makes him appear contemptible and almost ridiculous in her sight. Still she clings to him. She has no one else; she is alone among strangers. He belongs to her and she to him. This fact of their belonging to each other makes her tire of his company, and one day, when he and his literary friends are preparing to hold lectures in her drawing-room, she flies from the house to escape from their esthetic chatter.

At last she can stand it no longer, and whilst her guests are engaged in discussing a work of Mark's, she goes downstairs and out into the night. She scarcely knows what she is doing; her pulse beats feverishly, her nerves are quite unstrung. She walks down the street towards the Champs Elysées, and there she meets a man coming towards her. She perceives that she is alone in the empty street, and she is overcome with a nameless fear. Seized with a sudden impulse to hide herself, she jumps into the nearest cab, which is standing at the door of a café. The driver asks, "Where to?" and when she does not reply, he gets angry. At this juncture the man appears at the door of the carriage, and she recognizes Imre Borogh, a friend of Mark's, who was on his way to call on her. She still cannot say where she wishes to go, but feeling herself under the protection of a friend, she allows him to get in. They drive and drive. She perceives the compromising nature of the situation, but is too stupefied to put an end to it. He talks to her after the manner of an emotional young man, whose feelings have gained the mastery over him. At last he tells the driver to stop in front of a café. She is half unconscious, but he assists her to get out. And the nervous strain of these many long months results in a misunderstanding with this stranger, even greater than would have been the case with Mark.

She comes very quietly home. She takes hold of Mark's portrait, as she has so often done before, and compares it with her own image in the looking-glass. She throws it away. She burns his letters and all the little mementos which she has of him, then—while she is searching in her drawers—she comes upon a revolver....

Mark was very much moved at the funeral, and he cherished her memory for long afterwards.

Nowhere in the book is there any attempt made to describe men. The authoress only shows them to us as they are reflected in her soul. In this she not only shows an unusual amount of artistic talent, but also a new method. Woman is the most subjective of all creatures; she can only write about her own feelings, and her expression of them is her most valuable contribution to literature. Formerly women's writings were, for the most part, either directly or indirectly, the expression of a great falsehood. They were so overpoweringly impersonal, it was quite comic to see the way in which they imitated men's models, both in form and contents. Now that woman is conscious of her individuality as a woman, she needs an artistic mode of expression; she flings aside the old forms, and seeks for new. It is with this feeling, almost Bacchanalian in its intensity, that Mrs. Egerton hurls forth her playful stories, which the English critics judged harshly, but the public bought and called for in fresh editions; and this was how the Austrian lady wrote her story, which has the effect of a play dreamed under the influence of the sordine. Both books are honest. The more conscious a woman is of her individuality, the more honest will her confession be. Honesty is only another form of pride.

3

Another characteristic is beginning to make itself felt, which was bound to come at last. And that is an intense and morbid consciousness of the ego in women. This consciousness was unknown to our mothers and grandmothers; they may have had stronger characters than ours, as they undoubtedly had to overcome greater hindrances; but this consciousness of the ego is quite another thing, and they had not got it.

Neither of these women, whose books I have been reviewing, are authors by profession. There is nothing they care for less than to write books, and nothing that they desire less than to hear their names on every one's lips. Both were able to write without having learned. Other authoresses of whom we hear have either taught themselves to write, or have been taught by men. They began with an object, but without having anything to say; they chose their subjects from without.

Neither of these women have any object. They do not want to describe what they have seen. They do not want to teach the world, nor do they try to improve it. They have nothing to fight against. They merely put themselves into their books. They did not even begin with the intention of writing; they obeyed an impulse. There was no question of whether they wished or not; they were obliged. The moment came when they were forced to write, and they did not concern themselves with reasons or objects. Their ego burst forth with such power that it ignored all outer circumstances; it pressed forward and crystallized itself into an artistic shape. These women have not only a very pronounced style of their own, but are in fact artists; they became it as soon as they took up the pen. They had nothing to learn, it was theirs already.

This is not only a new phase in the work of literary production, it is also a new phase in woman's nature. Formerly, not only all great authoresses, but likewise all prominent women, were—or tried to be—intellectual. That also was an attempt to accommodate themselves to men's wishes. They were always trying to follow in the footsteps of the man. Man's ideas, interests, speculations, were to be understood and sympathized with. When philosophy was the fashion, great authoresses and intelligent women philosophized. Because Goethe was wise, Rahel was filled with the wisdom of life. George Eliot preached in all her books, and philosophized all her life long after the manner of Stuart Mill and Herbert Spencer. George Sand was the receptacle for ideas—men's ideas—of the most contradictory character, which she immediately reproduced in her novels. Good Ebner-Eschenbach writes as sensibly, and with as much tolerance, as a right worthy old gentleman; and Fru Leffler chose her subjects from among the problems which were being discussed by a few well-known men. None of their writings can be considered as essentially characteristic of women. It was not an altogether unjust assertion when men declared that the women who wrote books were only half women.

Yet these were the best. Others, who wrote as women, had no connection with literature at all; they merely knitted literary stockings.

Mrs. Egerton and the author of "Dilettantes" are not intellectual, not in the very least. The possibility of being it has never entered their brain. They had no ambition to imitate men. They are not in the least impressed by the speculations, ideas, theories, and philosophies of men. They are sceptics in all that concerns the mind; the man himself they can perceive.

They perceive his soul, his inner self,—when he has one,—and they are keenly sensitive when it is not there. The other women with the great names are quite thick-headed in comparison. They judge everything with the understanding; these perceive with the nerves, and that is an entirely different kind of understanding.

They understand man, but, at the same time, they perceive that he is quite different from themselves, that he is the contrast to themselves. The one is too highly cultured; the other has too sensitive a nervous system to permit the thought of any equality between man and woman. The idea makes them laugh. They are far too conscious of being refined, sensitive women. They do not concern themselves with the modern democratic tendencies regarding women, with its levelling of contrasts, its desire for equality. They live their own life, and if they find it unsatisfying, empty, disappointing, they cannot change it. But they do not make any compromise to do things by halves; their highly-developed nerves are too sure a standard to allow of that. They are a new race of women, more resigned, more hopeless, and more sensitive than the former ones. They are women such as the new men require; they have risen up on the intellectual horizon as the forerunners of a generation who will be more sensitive, and who will have a keener power of enjoyment than the former ones. Among themselves these women exchange sympathetic glances, and are able to understand one another without need of confession. They, with their highly-developed nerves, can feel for each other with a sympathy such as formerly a woman only felt for man. In this way they go through life, without building castles in the air, or making any plans for the future; they live on day by day, and never look beyond. It might be said that they are waiting; but as each new day arrives, and the sand of time falls drop by drop upon their delicate nerves, even this imperceptible burden is more than they can bear; the strain of it is too much for them.

4

I have before me a new book by Mrs. Egerton, and two new photographs. In the one she is sitting curled up in a chair, reading peacefully. She has a delicate, rather sharp-featured profile, with a long, somewhat prominent chin, that gives one an idea of yearning. The other is a full-length portrait. A slender, girlish figure, with narrow shoulders, and a waist, if anything, rather too small; a tired, worn face, without youth and full of disillusion; the hair looks as though restless fingers had been passed through it, and there is a bitter, hopeless expression about the lines of the mouth. In her letters—in which we never wholly possess her, but merely her *mood*—she comes to us in various guises,—now as a playful kitten, that is curled up cozily, and sometimes stretches out a soft little paw in playful, tender need of a caress; or else she is a worried, disappointed woman, with overwrought and excitable nerves, skeptical in the possibility of content, a seeker, for whom the charm lies in the seeking, not in the finding. She is a type of the modern woman, whose inmost being is the essence of disillusion.

When we examine the portraits of the four principal characters in this book—Sonia Kovalevsky, Eleonora Duse, Marie Bashkirtseff, and George Egerton—we find that they all have one feature in common. It was not I who first noticed this, it was a man. Ola Hansson, seeing them lying together one day, pointed it out to me, and he said: "The lips of all four speak the same language,—the young girl, the great tragedian, the woman of intellect, and the neurotic writer; each one has a something about the corners of the mouth that expresses a wearied satiety, mingled with an unsatisfied longing, as though she had as yet enjoyed nothing."

Why this wearied satiety mingled with an unsatisfied longing? Why should these four women, who are four opposites, as it were, have the same expression? The virgin in body and soul, the great creator of the roles of the degenerates, the mathematical professor, and the neurotic writer? Is it something in themselves, something peculiar in the organic nature of their womanhood, or is it some influence from without? Is it because they have chosen a profession which excites, while it leaves them dissatisfied, for the simple reason that a profession can never wholly satisfy a woman? Yet these four have excelled in their profession. But can a woman ever obtain satisfaction by means of her achievements? Is not her life as a woman—as a wife and as a mother—the true source of all her happiness? And this touch of disillusion in all of them—is it the disillusion they have experienced as *woman*; is it the expression of their bitter experiences in the gravest moment in a woman's life? Disappointment in man? *The* man that fate thrust across their path, who was their experience? And their yearning is now fruitless, for the flower of expectant realization withered before they plucked it.

Two of these women have carried the secret of their faces with them to the grave, but the others live and are not willing to reveal it. George Egerton would like to be as silent about it as they are; but her nerves speak, and her nerves have betrayed her secret in the book called "Discords."

When we read "Discords" we ask ourselves how is it possible that this frail little woman could write such a strong, brutal book? In "Keynotes" Mrs. Egerton was still a little coquette, with 5¾ gloves and 18-inch waist, who herself played a fascinating part. She had something of a midge's nature, dancing up and down, and turning nervous somersaults in the sunshine. "Discords" is certainly a continuation of "Keynotes," but it is quite another kind of woman who meets us here. The thrilling, nervous note of the former book has changed into a clashing, piercing sound, hard as metal; it is the voice of an accuser in whom all bitterness takes the form of reproaches which are unjust, and yet unanswerable. It is the voice of a woman who is conscious of being ill-treated and driven to despair, and who speaks in spite of herself in the name of thousands of ill-treated and despairing women. Who can tell us whether her nerves have ill-treated this woman and driven her to despair, or whether it is her outward fate, especially her fate with regard to the man? Women of this kind are not confidential. They take back to-morrow what they have confessed to-day, partly from a wish not to let themselves be understood, and partly because the aspect of their experiences varies with every change of mood, like the colors in a kaleidoscope.

But throughout these changes, one single note is maintained in "Discords," as it was in "Keynotes." In the latter it was a high, shrill treble, like the song of a bird in spring; in "Discords" it is a deep bass note, groaning in distress with the groan of a disappointed woman.

5

The tone of bitter disappointment which pervades "Discords" is the expression of woman's disappointment in man. Man and man's love are not a joy to her; they are a torment. He is inconsiderate in his demands, brutal in his caresses, and unsympathetic with those sides of her nature which are not there for his satisfaction. He is no longer the great comic animal of "Keynotes," whom the woman teases and plays with—he is a nightmare which smothers her during horrible nights, a hangman who tortures her body and soul during days and years for his pleasure; a despot who demands admiration, caresses, and devotion, while her every nerve quivers with an opposite emotion; a man born blind, whose clumsy fingers press the spot where the pain is, and when she moans, replies with coarse, unfeeling laughter, "Absurd nonsense!"

Although I believed myself to be acquainted with all the books which women have written against men, no book that I have ever read has impressed me with such a vivid sense of physical pain. Most women come with reasonings, moral sermons, and outbursts of temper: a man may allow himself much that is forbidden to others, that must be altered. Women are of no importance in his eyes; he has permitted himself to look down upon them. They intend to teach him their importance. They are determined that he shall look up to them. But here we have no trace of Xantippe-like violence, only a woman who holds her trembling hands to the wounds which man has inflicted upon her, of which the pain is intensified each time that he draws near. A woman, driven to despair, who jumps upon him like a wild-cat, and seizes him by the throat; and if that does not answer, chooses for herself a death that is ten times more painful than life with him, *chooses* it in order that she may have her own way.

What is this? It is not the well-known domestic animal which we call woman. It is a wild creature belonging to a wild race, untamed and untamable, with the yellow gleam of a wild animal in its eyes. It is a nervous, sensitive creature, whose primitive wildness is awakened by a blow which it has received, which bursts forth, revengeful and pitiless as the lightning in the night.

That is what I like about this book. That a woman should have sprung up, who with her instinct can bore to the bottom layers of womanhood the quality that enables her to renew the race, her primeval quality, which man, with all his understanding, has never penetrated. A few years ago, in a study on Gottfried Keller's women, I mentioned wildness as the basis of woman's nature; Mrs. Egerton has given utterance to the same opinion in "Keynotes," and has since tried to embody it in "Discords;" her best stories are those where the wild instinct breaks loose.

But why this terror of man, this physical repulsion, as in the story called "Virgin Soil"? The authoress says that it is because an ignorant girl in her complete innocence is handed over in marriage to an exacting husband. But that is not reason enough. The authoress's intellect is not as true as her instinct. There must be something more. The same may be said of "Wedlock," where the boarding-house cook marries an amorous working man, who is in receipt of good wages, for the sake of having her illegitimate child to live with her; he refuses to allow it, and when the child dies of a childish ailment, she murders his two children by the first marriage.

Mrs. Egerton's stories are not invented; neither are they realistic studies copied from the notes in her diary. They are experiences. She has lived them all, because the people whom she portrays have impressed their characters or their fate upon her quivering nerves. The music of her nerves has sounded like the music of a stringed instrument beneath the touch of a strange hand, as in that masterpiece, "Gone Under," where the woman tells her story between the throes of sea-sickness and drunkenness. The man to whom she belongs has punished her unfaithfulness by the murder of her child, and she revenges herself by drunkenness; yet, in spite of it all, he remains the master whom she is powerless to punish, and in her despair she throws herself upon the streets.

Only one man has had sufficient instinct to bring to light this abyss in woman's nature, and that is Barbey d'Aurevilly, the poet who was never understood. But in Mrs. Egerton's book there is one element which he had not discovered, and, although she does not express it in words, it shows itself in her description of men and women. Her men are Englishmen with bull-dog natures, but the women belong to another race; and is not this horror, this physical repulsion, this woman raging against the man, a true representation of the way that the Anglo-Saxon nature reacts upon the Celtic?

Two races stand opposed to one another in these sketches; perhaps the authoress herself is not quite conscious of it, but it is plainly visible in her descriptions of character, where we have the heavy, massive Englishman, *l'animal mâle*, and the untamable woman who is prevented by race instinct from loving where she ought to love.

In "The Regeneration of Two," Mrs. Egerton has tried to describe a Celtic woman where she can love, but the attempt is most unsuccessful, for here we see plainly that she lacked the basis of experience. There are, however, many women who know what love is, although they have never experienced it. Men came, they married, but the man for them never came.

6

There is a little story in this collection called "Her Share," where the style is full of tenderness, perhaps even a trifle too sweet. It affects one like a landscape on an evening in early autumn, when the sun has gone down and twilight reigns; it seems as though veiled in gray, for there is no color left, although everything is strangely clear. Mrs. Egerton has a peculiarly gentle touch and soft voice where she describes the lonely, independent working girl. Her little story is often nothing more than the fleeting shadow of a mood, but the style is sustained throughout in a warm stream of lyric; for this Celtic woman certainly has the lyrical faculty, a thing which a woman writer rarely has, if ever, possessed before. There is something in her writing which seems to express a desire to draw near to the lonely girl and say: "You have such a good time of it in your grayness. In Grayness your nerves find rest, your instincts slumber, no man ill-treats you with his love, you experience discontent in contentment, but you know nothing of the torture of unstrung nerves. Would I were like you; but I am a bundle of electric currents bursting forth in all directions into chaos."

Besides these two dainty twilight sketches, she has others like the description in "Gone Under," of the storm on that voyage from America to England where we imagine ourselves on board ship, and seem to feel the rolling sea, to hear the ship cracking and groaning, to smell the hundreds of fetid smells escaping from all corners, and the damp ship-biscuits and the taste of the bitter salt spray on the tongue. We owe this forcible and matter-of-fact method of reproducing the impressions received by the senses to the retentive power of her nerves, through which she is able to preserve her passing impressions and to reproduce them in their full intensity. She relies on her womanly receptive faculty, not on her brain.

*****

George Egerton's life has been of the kind which affords ample material for literary purposes, and it is probable that she has more raw material ready for use at any time when she may require it; but at present she retains it in her nerves, as it were, under lock and key. She had intended from childhood to become an artist, and writing is only an afterthought; yet, no sooner did she begin to write than the impressions and experiences of her life shaped themselves into the form of her two published works. Until the publication of "Discords," we had thought that she was one of those intensely individualistic writers who write one book because they must, but never write another, or, at any rate, not one that will bear comparison with the first; the publication of "Discords" has entirely dispelled this opinion, and has given us good reason to hope for many more works from her pen.

The Modern Woman on
the Stage

1

A lean figure, peculiarly attractive, though scarcely to be called beautiful; a melancholy face with a strangely sweet expression, no longer young, yet possessed of a pale, wistful charm; *la femme de trente ans*, who has lived and suffered, and who knows that life is full of suffering; a woman without any aggressive self-confidence, yet queenly, gentle, and subdued in manner, with a pathetic voice,—such is Eleonora Duse as she appeared in the parts which she created for herself out of modern pieces. When first I saw her, I tried to think of some one with whom to compare her; I turned over in my mind the names of all the greatest actresses in the last ten years or more, and wondered whether any of them could be said to be her equal, or to have surpassed her. But neither Wolter nor Bernhardt, neither Ellmenreich nor the best actresses of the *Théâtre Français*, could be compared with her. The French and German actresses were entirely different; they seemed to stand apart, each complete in themselves—while she too stood apart, complete in herself. They represented a world of their own and a perfected civilization; and she, though like them in some ways, seemed to represent the genesis of a world, and a civilization in embryo. This was not merely the result of comparing an Italian with French and German, and one school with another,—it was the woman's temperament compared to that of others, her acute susceptibility, compared to which her celebrated predecessors impressed one as being too massive, almost too crude, and one might be tempted to add, less womanly. Many of them have possessed a more versatile genius than hers, and nearly all have had greater advantages at their disposal; but the moment that we compare them to Duse, their loud, convulsive art suddenly assumes the appearance of one of those gigantic pictures by Makart, once so fiery colored and now so faded; and if we compare the famous dramatic artists of the seventies and eighties with Duse, we might as well compare a splendid festal march played with many instruments to a Violin solo floating on the still night air.

The pieces acted by Eleonora Duse at Berlin, where I saw her, were mainly chosen to suit the public taste, and they differed in nothing from the usual virtuosa program. These consisted of Sarah Bernhardt's favorite parts, such as "Fédora," "La Dame aux Camélias," and pieces taken from the *répertoire* of the *Théâtre Français*, such as "Francillon" and "Divorçons," varied with "Cavalleria Rusticana," and such well-known plays as "Locandiera," "Fernande," and "The Doll's House." She did not act Shakespeare, and there she was wise; for what can Duse's pale face have in common with the exuberant spirits and muscular strength of the women of the *Renaissance*, whose own rich life-blood shone red before their eyes and drove them to deeds of love and vengeance, which it makes the ladies of our time ill to hear described. But she also neglected some pieces which must have suited her better than her French *répertoire*. She did not give us Marco Praga's "Modest Girls," where Paulina's part seems expressly created for her, nor his "Ideal Wife," into which she might have introduced some of her own instinctive philosophy. Neither did she act the "Tristi Amori" of her celebrated fellow-countryman, Giuseppe Giacosa.

And yet, in the parts which she did act, she opened to us a new world, which had no existence before, because it was her own. It was the world of her own soul, the ever-changing woman's world, which no one before her has ever expressed on the stage; she gave us the secret, inner life of woman, which no poet can wholly fathom, and which only woman herself can reveal, which with more refined nerves and more sensitive and varied feelings has emerged bleeding from the older, coarser, narrower forms of art, to newer, brighter forms, which, though more powerful, are also more wistful and more hopeless.

2

Eleonora Duse has a strangely wearied look. It is not the weariness of exhaustion or apathy, nor is it the weariness natural to an overworked actress, although there are times when she suffers from that to so great an extent that she acts indifferently the whole evening, and makes the part a failure. Neither is it the weariness of despondency which gives the voice a hollow, artificial sound, which is noticeable in all virtuosas when they are over-tired. Neither is it the utter prostration resulting from passion, like the drowsiness of beasts of prey, which our tragic actors and actresses delight in. Passion, the so-called great passion, which, according to an old legend recounted in one of the Greek tragedies, comes like the whirlwind, and leaves nothing behind but death and dried bones—passion such as that is unknown to Duse. Brunhild, Medea, Messalina, and all the ambitious, imperious princesses of historic drama are nothing to her; she is no princess or martyr of ancient history, but a princess in her own right, and a martyr of circumstances. Throughout her acting there is a feeling of surprise that she should suffer and be martyred, accompanied by the dim knowledge that it must be so—and it is that which gives her soul its weary melancholy. For it is not her body, nor her senses, nor her mind which give the appearance of having just awoke from a deep lethargy; the weariness is all in her soul, and it is that which gives her a soft, caressing, trustful manner, as though she felt lonely, and yearned for a little sympathy. Love is full of sympathy, and that is why Eleonora Duse acts love. Not greedy love, which asks more than it gives, like Walter's and Bernhardt's; not sensual love, nor yet imperious love, like the big woman who takes pity on the little man, whom it pleases her to make happy. When Duse is in love, even in "Fédora," it is always she who is the little woman, and the man is for her the big man, the giver, who holds her happiness in his hands, to whose side she steals anxiously, almost timidly, and looks up at him with her serious, wearied, almost child-like smile. She comes to him for protection and shelter, just as travelers are wont to gather round a warm fire, and she clings to him caressingly with her thin little hands,—the hands of a child and mother. Never has woman been represented in a more womanly way than by Eleonora Duse; and more than that, I take it upon myself to maintain that woman has never been represented upon the stage until now—by Eleonora Duse.

She shows us the everlasting child in woman,—in the full-grown, experienced woman, who is possessed of an erotic yearning for fulness of life. Woman is not, and cannot be, happy by herself, nor is the sacrifice of a moment enough for her; it is not enough for her to live by the side of the man; a husband's tenderness is as necessary to her as the air she breathes. His passion, lit by her, is her life and happiness. He gives her the love in which her life can blossom into a fair and beautiful flower. And she accepts him, not with the silly innocence of a child, not with the ignorance of girlhood, not with the ungoverned passion of a mistress, not with the condescending forbearance of the "superior woman," not with the brotherly affection of the manly woman,—we have had ample opportunity of seeing and benefiting by such representations as those in every theatre, and in every tongue, since first we began to see and to think. They include every type of womanhood as understood and represented by actresses great and small. But into all this, Duse introduces a new element, something which was formerly only a matter of secondary importance on the stage, which, by the "highest art," was judged in the light of a juggler's trick, and was considered by the lower art as little more than a valuable ingredient. She makes it the main-string on which her acting vibrates, the keynote without which her art would have no meaning. She accepts the man with the whole-hearted sincerity of an experienced woman, who shrinks from the loneliness of life, and longs to lose herself in the "loved one". She has the dreadful sensation that a human being has nothing but minutes, minutes; that there is nothing lasting to rely on; that we swim across dark waters from yesterday until to-morrow, and our unfulfilled desires are less terrible than the feverish anxiety with which we anticipate the future in times of prosperity.

Eleonora Duse's acting tells of infinite suspense.

Her entire art rests on this one note,—Suspense: which means that we know nothing, possess nothing, can do nothing; that everything is ruled by chance, and the whole of life is one great uncertainty. This terrible insecurity stands as a perfect contrast to the "cause and effect" theory of the schools, which trust in God and logic, and offer a secure refuge to the playwright's art. This mysterious darkness, from whence she steps forward like a sleep-walker, gives a sickly coloring to her actions. There is something timid about her; she seems to have an almost superstitious dislike of a shrill sound, or a brilliant color; and this peculiarity of hers finds expression not only in her acting, but also in her dress.

We seldom see toilets on the stage which reveal a more individual taste. Just as Duse never acted anything but what was in her own soul, she never attempted any disguise of her body. Her own face was the only mask she wore when I saw her act. The expression of her features, the deep lines on her cheeks, the melancholy mouth, the sunken eyes with their large heavy lids, were all characteristic of the part. She always had the same black, broad, arched eyebrows, the same wavy, shiny black Italian hair, which was always done up in a modest knot, sometimes high, sometimes a little lower, from which two curls always escaped during the course of her acting, because she had a habit of brushing her forehead with a white and rather bony hand, as though every violent emotion made her head ache.

No jewel glittered against her sallow skin, and she wore no ornament on her dress; there was something pathetic in the unconcealed thinness of her neck and throat. She was of medium height, a slender body with broad hips, without any signs of the rounded waist which belongs to the fashionable figure of the drama. She wore no stays, and there was nothing to hinder the slow, graceful, musical movements of her somewhat scanty figure. She made frequent gestures with her arms which were perfectly natural in her, although her Italian vivacity sometimes gave them a grotesque appearance. But it was the grace of her form, rather than her gestures, which called attention to the natural stateliness of her person. As to her dresses, they were not in the least fashionable, there was nothing of the French fashion-plate style about them; but then she never made any attempt to follow the fashion,—she set it. There was an antique look about the long soft folds of her dress, also something suggestive of the *Renaissance* in the velvet bodices and low lace collars.

But her arrangement of color was new; it was not copied either from the antique or the *Renaissance*, and it was certainly not in accordance with the present-day fashion. She never wore red,—with the exception of Nora's shabby blouse,—nor bright yellow, nor blue; never, in fact, any strong, deep color. The hues which she affected most were black and white in all materials, whether for dresses or cloaks. She always wore pale, cream-colored lace, closely folded across her breast, from whence her dress fell loosely to the ground; she never wore a waist-band of any kind whatever.

She sometimes wore pale bronze, faded violet, and quiet myrtle green in soft materials of velvet and silk. There was an air of mourning about her dresses which might have suited any age except merry youth, and that note was entirely absent from her art, for she was never merry. She had a happy look sometimes, but she was never merry or noisy on the stage. I have twice seen her in a hat; and they were sober hats, such as a widow might wear.

3

I saw Duse for the first time as "Nora."[2] I was sorry for it, as I did not think that an Italian could act the part of a heroine with such an essentially northern temperament. I have never had an opportunity of seeing Frau Ramlo, who is considered the best Nora on the German stage, but I have seen Ibsen's Nora, Fru Hennings of the Royal Theatre of Copenhagen, and I retained a vivid picture of her acting in my mind. Fru Hennings' Nora was a nervous little creature, with fair hair and sharp features, very neat and *piquante*, but dressed cheaply and not always with the best taste; she was the regular tradesman's daughter, with meagre purse and many pretensions, whose knowledge of life was bounded by the narrow prejudices of the parlor. There was something undeveloped about this Nora, with her senseless chatter, something almost pitiable in her admiration for the self-important Helmer, and something childish in her conception of his hidden heroism. There was also a natural, and perhaps inherited tendency for dishonest dealings, and a well-bred, forced cheerfulness which took the form of hopping and jumping in a coquettish manner, because she knew that it became her. When the time comes that she is obliged to face life with its realities, her feeble brain becomes quite confused, and she hops round the room in her tight stays, with her fringe and high-heeled boots, till, nervous and void of self-control as she is, she excites herself into the wildest apprehensions. This apprehension was the masterpiece of Fru Hennings' masterly acting. She kept the mind fixed on a single point, which had all the more powerful effect in that it was so characteristically depicted,—she showed us the way by which a respectable tradesman's daughter may be driven to the madhouse or to suicide. But when the change takes place, and a fully developed, argumentative, woman's rights woman jumps down upon the little goose, then even Fru Hennings' undoubted art was not equal to the occasion. The part fell to pieces, and two Noras remained, connected only by a little thread,—the miraculous. Fru Hennings disappears with an unspoken *au revoir!*

When Eleonora Duse comes upon the stage as Nora, she is a pale, unhealthy-looking woman, with a very quiet manner. She examines her purse thoughtfully, and before paying the servant she pauses involuntarily, as poor people usually do before they spend money. And when she throws off her shabby fur cloak and fur cap, she appears as a thin, black-haired Italian woman, clad in an old, ill-fitting red blouse. She plays with the children, without any real gayety, as grown-up people are in the habit of playing when their thoughts are otherwise occupied. Fru Linden enters, and to her she tells her whole history with true Italian volubility, but in an absent manner, like a person who is not thinking of what she is saying. She likes best to sit on the floor—very unlike women of her class—and to busy herself with the Christmas things. In the scene with Helmer an expression of submissive tenderness comes over her, she likes to be with him, she feels as though his presence afforded her protection, and she nestles to his side, more like a sick person than a child.

The scenes which are impressed with Nora's modern nervousness come and go, but Duse never becomes nervous. The many emotional and sudden changes which take place, the unreasonable actions and other minor peculiarities of a child of the *bourgeois décadence,*—these do not concern her. Duse never acts the nervous woman, either here or elsewhere. She does not act it, because she has too true and delicate a nervous susceptibility. She can act the most passionate feelings, and she often does so; but she never acts a capricious, nervous disposition. She has too refined a taste for that, and her soul is too full of harmony.

Ibsen's Nora is hysterical, and only half a woman; and that is what he, with his poetic intuition, intended her to be. Eleonora Duse's Nora is a complete woman. Crushed by want and living in narrow surroundings, there is a certain obtuseness about her which renders her willing to subject herself to new misfortunes. There is also something of the child in her, as there is in every true woman; but even in her child-like moments she is a sad child. Then the misfortune happens! But, strange to say, she makes no desperate attempt to resist it; she gives no hysterical cry of fear, as a meaner soul would do in the struggle for life. There is something pitiable in a struggle such as that, where power and will are so disproportionately unlike. Duse's Nora hastily suppresses the first suggestion of fear; but she does not admire her muff meanwhile, like Fru Hennings. She merely repeats to herself over and over again in answer to her thoughts: "No, no!" I never heard any one say "no" like her; it contains a whole world of human feeling. But all through the night she hears fate say "Yes, yes!" and the next day, which is Christmas Day, she is overcome with a fatalistic feeling. She dresses herself for the festival, but not with cheap rags like Nora; she wears an expensive dark green dress, which hangs down in rich graceful folds. It is her only best dress, and sets off her figure to perfection; it makes her look tall and slender, but also very weary. And as the play goes on, she becomes even more weary and more resigned, and when death comes, there is no help for it. Then, after the rehearsal of the tarantella, when Helmer calls to her from the dining-room and she knows that fate can no longer be averted, she leaps through the air into his arms with a cry of joy,—to look at her one would think that she was one of those thin, wild, joy-less Bacchantes whose bas-reliefs have come down to us from the later period of Grecian art.

The third act:—Nora and Helmer return from the mask ball. She is absent-minded and quite indifferent to everything that goes on around her. That which she knows is going to happen, is to her already a thing of the past, since she has endured it all in anticipation; her actions in the matter are only mechanical.

When Helmer goes to empty the letter-box, she does not try to stop him with a hundred excuses, she scarcely makes a weak movement to hold him back; she knows that it must come, nothing that she can do will prevent it. While Helmer reads the letter, she stands pale and motionless, and when he rushes at her, she throws on her mantle and leaves the room without another word.

He drags her back and overwhelms her with reproaches, in which the pitiful meanness of his soul is laid bare. Now Duse's acting begins in earnest, now the dramatic moment has come—the only moment in the drama—for the sake of which she took the part.

She stands by the fireplace, with her face towards the audience, and does not move a muscle until he has finished speaking. She says noth-ing, she never interrupts him. Only her eyes speak. He runs backwards and forwards, up and down the room, while she follows him with her large, suffering eyes, which have an unnatural look in them, follows him backwards and forwards in unutterable surprise,—a surprise which seems to have fallen from heaven, and which changes little by little into an unutterable, inconceivable disappointment, and that again into an indescribably bitter, sickening contempt. And into her eyes comes at last the question: "Who are you? What have you got to do with me? What do you want here? What are you talking about?"

The other letter drops into the letter-box, and Helmer loads her with tender, patronizing words. But she does not hear him. She is no longer looking at him. What does the chattering creature want now? She does not know him at all. She has never loved him. There was once a man whose sympathy she possessed, and who was her protector. That man is no more, and she has never loved any one!

She turns away with a gesture of displeasure, and goes to change her clothes, anxious to get away as quickly as possible. He stops her. What then? The woman is awake in her. She is a woman in the moment of a woman's greatest ignominy,—when she discovers that she does not love. What does he want with her? Why does he raise objections? He——? *Tant de bruit pour une omelette!* She throws him a few indifferent words, shrugs her shoulders, turns her back upon him, and goes quickly out at the door. Presently we hear the front door close with a bang. There is no mention at all about the "miracle."

That is how Duse united Nora's double personality. Make it up! There is no making it up between the man and wife, except the kiss and the shrug of the shoulders. She ignores Ibsen's principal argument. Reason, indeed? Reason has never settled anything in stern reality, least of all as regards the relationship between husband and wife. One day Nora wakes up and finds that Helmer has become loathsome to her, and she runs away from him with the instinctive horror of a living person for a decomposed corpse. Of course nothing "miraculous" can happen, for that would mean that the living person should go mad and return to the corpse.

Eleonora Duse treats all her parts in the same independent manner that she treats the text of Nora. When we are able to follow her, and that is by no means always, we notice how she alters it to suit herself, how another being comes to the front,—a being who has no place in the written words, and whom the author never thought of, whom he, in most cases, could certainly not have drawn from his own views of life and his own inner consciousness. Duse's heroine is more womanly, in the deeper sense of the word, than the society ladies in Ibsen's and Sardou's dramas, and she is not only more simple than they are, but also far greater. Eleonora Duse is not a dialectician like Ibsen and Sardou; their hair-splitting logic is no concern of hers, and it certainly was not written for her. She has an instinctive, unerring intuition of what the part should be, and she throws herself into it and acts accordingly. She does not vary much; she is not a realist who makes a careful note of every little peculiarity, and arranges them in a pattern of mosaic; she is truthful to a reckless extent, but not always true to the letter; some-times like this, sometimes like that, she differs in the different parts. She is true, because she is proud and courageous enough to show herself as she really is. There is no need for her to be otherwise. There is danger of uniformity in this great simplicity of hers, and she would not escape it if it were not for her emotional nature, and an intense, almost painful sincerity, which was perhaps never represented on the stage before her time, and which was certainly never before made the groundwork of a woman's feelings. She comes to meet us half absorbed in her own thoughts, a complete woman,—complete in that indissoluble unity which is the basis of a healthy woman's nature: woman-child and also woman-mother, a woman with the stamp which is the result of deep, vital experience, with a woman's tragedy ineffaceably engraved on every feature,—this same woman's tragedy which she reproduces upon the stage. It is the fact of her not troubling herself about anything else that imbues her acting with an air of simplicity, and because she is such a complete woman herself, there is an air of indescribable stateliness about her acting. She not only simplified all that she took in hand, but she also improved it. For all these characters which she created were the result of the completeness of her womanly nature, and that is why they never had but the one motive, for all the evil they did, and for their hate: they revenged themselves for the *crimen læsæ majestatis*, which sin was committed against their womanly nature, and which a true woman never forgives, as when the priceless pearl of her womanhood has been misused. That is why they made no pathetic gestures, no noise or tragic screams, but acted quietly and silently, as we do a thing which is ex-pected of us, with a quiet indifference, as when intact nature bows itself under and assists fate.

That is how Duse acted Nora, but she acted Clotilde in "Fernande" in the same mood, also Odette in the play, called by the same name, both by Sardou, and that was more difficult. Clotilde and Odette are a couple of vulgar people. Clotilde, a widow of distinction, revenges her-self upon a young man of proud and noble family, who has been her lover for many years, but has broken his marriage vows, by encouraging his attachment for a dishonored girl, whom she persuades him to marry, and afterwards triumphantly tells him his wife's history.

Odette's husband finds her one night with her lover, and he turns her out of the house in the presence of witnesses. For several years she leads a dissolute life, dishonoring the name of her husband and grown-up daughter. This stain on the family makes it almost impossible for the latter to marry, and the husband offers the fallen woman a large sum of money to deprive her of his name. She agrees, on condition that she shall be allowed to see her daughter. She is prevented from making herself known to the latter, and when she comes away after the interview, she drowns herself in a fit of hysterical self-contempt. Such are the contents of the two pieces into which Duse put her greatest and best talent.

4

She comes as Clotilde into the gambling saloon, to inquire after the young girl whom she had nearly driven over. She is simply dressed, and has the appearance of a distinguished lady, with a happy and virtuous past. The manner in which she receives the girl in her own house, talks to her and puts her at her ease, was so kind and hearty that the audience, very unexpectedly in this scene, broke into a storm of applause before the curtain had gone down. Her lover returns from a journey which arouses her suspicion, and she, anxious not to deceive herself, elicits the confession that he no longer cares for her, and is in love with some one else. That some one is Fernande. He goes to look for her, finds her in the same house, and returns immediately. Clotilde thinks that he has come back to her. Her speechless delight must be seen, for it cannot be described; her whole being is suffused with a radiant joy, she trembles with excitement. When it is all made plain to her, and there is no longer any room for doubt, she bows her head over his hand for an instant, as though to kiss it, as she had so often done before, then she strokes it softly with her own.... She will never look into his face again, yet she cannot cease to love the clear, caressing hand, which calls to mind her former happiness.

She lets things take their course, and when it is over she has the scene with Pomerol, when she defends her conduct. Duse has a form of dialectic peculiar to herself, which is neither sensible nor deliberate, but impulsive. When she does wrong she does it—not because she is bad, but because she cannot help herself. A part of her nature, which was the source of her life, is wounded and sick unto death, and a gnawing, burning pain compels her to commit deeds as dark and painful as her own heart. She goes about it quietly, doing it all as a matter of course; to her they seem inevitable as the outer expression of a hidden suffering.

She is at her best in the passionate "Fédora," when she represents this state of blank amazement, mingled with despair, taking the place of what has been love. If she afterwards comes across the French cynic, she reasons with him too—but like a woman, *i.e.*, she drowns his arguments in an extraordinary number of interjections, with or without words. She never crosses the threshold of her life as an actress, she never once attains to the consciousness of objective judgment.

When the man whom she loves is married to the dishonored girl, Clotilde comes to bring him the information which she has reserved until now. Suddenly she stands in the doorway, and sees that he is alone, and there comes over her an indescribable expression of dumb, suppressed love. She seems to be making a frantic appeal to the past to be as though it had never taken place, and in the emotion of the moment she has forgotten what brought her there. Not until he has unceremoniously shown her the door, and opened the old wound, does she tell him who his wife is.

The same with "Odette." She is in love, and she receives her lover. At that moment her husband comes home. (Andó, Duse's partner, is almost as good an actor as she is.) He is a shallow, restless, hot-tempered little man, who seizes her by the shoulders as she is about to throw herself into the other man's arms. She collapses altogether, and stands before him stammering and ashamed. He thrusts her out of the house, although it is the middle of the night, and she is lightly clad. In a moment she has drawn herself up to her full height,—a woman deprived of home and child, on whom the deadliest injury has been inflicted in the most barbarous manner; in the presence of such cruelty, her own fault sinks to nothing, and with a voice as hoarse as that of an animal at bay, she cries, "Coward!" and leaves him.

Many years have gone by, and we meet Odette once more, this time as a courtesan in a gambling saloon. She is very much aged,—a thin, disillusioned woman, for whom her husband is searching everywhere, with the intention of depriving her of his name. There is still something about her which bears the impress of the injured woman. She recalls the past as clearly as though it happened only yesterday; for she can never forget it, and time has not lessened the disgrace. She treats him with wearied indifference, and her voice is harsh like an animal's, and she chokes as though she were trying to smother her indignation.

Then follows the last act, when she meets her daughter. She comes in, dressed like an unhappy old widow, shaking with emotion, and scarcely able to contain herself. Her eyes are aglow with excitement, as she rushes forward, ready to cast herself into her daughter's arms. But when she sees the fresh, innocent girl, she is overcome with a feeling of shyness, and shrinks from her with an awkward, anxious gesture. She speaks hesitatingly, like one who is ill at ease; she raises her shoulders and stoops, and holds her thin, restless hands clasped together, lest they should touch her daughter. The girl displays the various little souvenirs that belonged to her mother, and plays the piece which was her favorite, and talks about her "dead mother." Then this man and woman are stirred with a deep feeling, which is the simple keynote of humanity, which they never experienced before in the days when they were together. And they sit and cry, each buried in their own sorrow, and far apart from one another. After that she puts her trembling arms round the girl, and kisses her with an expression in her face which it is impossible to simulate, and which cannot be imitated,—which no one understands except the woman who is herself a mother. She gazes at her daughter as though she could never see enough of her; she strokes her with feverish hands, arranges the lace on her dress, and you feel the joy that it is to her to touch the girl, and to know that she is really there. Then she becomes very quiet, as though she had suffered all that it was possible for her to suffer. As she passes her husband, she catches hold of his outstretched hand, and tries to kiss it. Then she tears herself away, overcome with the feeling that she can endure it no longer.

Eleonora Duse prefers difficult parts. She was nothing more than an ordinary actress in "La Locandiera," and the witty dialogue in "Cyprienne" and "Francillon" had little in common with her nature. Even the part of "La Dame aux Camélias" was an effort to her. The silly, frivolous cocotte, with her consumptive longing to be loved, was too exaggerated a part for Eleonora Duse. A superabundance of good spirits is foreign to her nature, which is sad as life itself. Pride and arrogance she cannot act, nor yet the trustfulness which comes from inexperience. She gave the impression of not feeling young enough for "La Dame aux Camélias'" happy and unhappy moods. Eleonora Duse's art is most at home where life's great enigma begins:—Where do we come from? Why are we here?

Where are we going to? We are tossed to and fro on the waters in a dense fog; we suffer wrong, and we do wrong, and we know not why. Fate! fate! We are powerless in the hands of Fate! When Duse can act the blindness of fatalism, then she is content.

She was able to do so in "Fédora."

The pretty, fashionable heroine does not change into a fury when the man whom she loves is brought home murdered. When we meet her again she is quite quiet,—a calm, cold woman of the world, with only one object in life, which is to punish the murderer. It is a task like any other, but it is inevitable, and must be undertaken as a matter of course. She makes no display of anger, and takes no perverse pleasure in thoughts of vengeance. The murderer is nothing to her,—he is a stranger. But she has been rendered desolate in the flower of her youth; the table of life, which is never spread more than once, has been upset before her eyes at the very moment of her anticipated happiness, and this is an injury which she is going to repay. She is proud, and has no illusions; she is a just judge, who recompenses evil with evil and good with good. This "Fédora" is reserved and unreasoning.

The scene changes. She loves the man whom she has been pursuing, and she discovers that the dead man has been false to both of them, and she realizes that now for the first time life's table is spread for her, while the secret police, to whom she has betrayed him, are waiting outside, and she clings to him terrified, showers caresses upon him, kisses him with unspeakable tenderness. There is something in her of the help-lessness of a little child, mingled with a mother's protecting care, as she implores him to remain, and entices him to love, and seeks refuge in his love, as a terrified animal seeks refuge in its hole.

There are two other features of Eleonora Duse's art which deserve notice. These are, the way in which she tells a lie, and the way she acts death. As I have said already, she is not a realist, and she frames her characters from her inner consciousness, not from details gathered from the outward features of life. Her representation of death is also the outcome of her instinct. A death scene has no meaning for her unless it reflects the inner life. As a process of physical dissolution, she takes no interest in it. She has not studied death from the side of the sick-bed, and she makes short work of it in "Fédora," as also in "La Dame aux Camélias." In the first piece, the point which she emphasizes is the sudden determination to take the poison; in the second, it is her joy at having the man whom she loves near her at the last.

Then her manner of lying. When Duse tells a lie, she does it as if it were the simplest and most natural thing in the world. Her lies and deceptions are as engaging, persuasive, and fantastic as a child's. Lying is an important factor in the character of a woman who has much to fight against, and it is a weapon which she delights to use, and the use of it renders her unusually fascinating and affectionate. Even those who do not understand the words of the play, know when Duse is telling a lie, because she becomes so unusually lively and talkative, and her large eyes have an irresistible sparkle in them.

"Cavalleria Rusticana" was the only good Italian play that Duse acted. She was more of a realist in this piece than in any other, because she reproduced what she had seen daily before her eyes,—her native surroundings, her fellow-countrymen,—instead of that which she had learned by listening to her own soul. Her Santuzza—the poor, forsaken girl with the raw, melancholy, guttural accents of despair—was life-like and convincing, but the barbaric wildness of the exponent was some-thing which was as startling in this stupid, pale weakly creature as a roar from the throat of a roe deer.

5

And now to sum up:—Eleonora Duse goes touring all round the world. She is going to America, and she is certain to go back to Berlin and St. Petersburg and Vienna, and other places where she may or may not have been before. She will have to travel and act, travel and act, as all popular actresses have done before her. She will grow tired of it, unspeakably tired,—we can see that already,—but she will be obliged to go on, till she becomes stereotyped, like all the others.

When we see her again, will she be the same as she is now? Her technical power is extraordinary, but her art is simple; melancholy and dignity are its chief ingredients. Will Duse's womanly nature be able to bear the strain of never-ending repetition? This fear has been the cause of my endeavor to accentuate her individuality as it appeared to me when I saw her. Hers is not one of those powerful natures which always regain their strength, and are able to fight through all difficulties. Her entire acting is tuned upon one note, which is usually nothing more than an accompaniment in the art of acting; that note is sincerity. In my opinion she is the greatest woman genius on the stage.

Nowadays we are either too lavish or too sparing in our use of the word genius; we either brandish it abroad with every trumpet, or else avoid it altogether. We are willing to allow that there are geniuses amongst actors and actresses, and that such have existed, and may perhaps continue to exist, but I have never observed that any attempt is made to distinguish between the genius of man and woman on the stage. This may possibly be accounted for by the fact that the difference was not great. The hero was manly, the heroine womanly, and the old people, whether men or women, were either comic or tearful, and the characters of both sexes were usually bad. The difference lay chiefly in the dress, the general comportment, and the voice: one could see which was the woman, and she of course acted a woman's feelings; tradition ruled, and in accordance with it the actress imitated the man, declaimed her part like him, and even went as far as to imitate the well-known tragic step. Types, not individuals, were represented on the stage, and I have seldom seen even the greatest actresses of the older school deviate from this rule.

The society pieces were supposed to represent every-day life; therefore it was necessary before all else that the actress should be a lady, and where a lady's feelings are limited, hers were necessarily limited too. To every actress, the tragedian not excepted, the question of chief importance was how she looked.

But Duse does not care in the least how she looks. Her one desire is to find means of expressing an emotion of the soul which overwhelms her, and is one of the mysteries of her womanly nature. Her acting is not realistic; by which I mean that she does not attempt to impress her audience by making her acting true to life, which can be easily attained by means of pathological phenomena, such as a cough, the cramp, a death-struggle, etc., which are really the most expressive, and also, in a coarse way, the most successful. She will have none of this, because it is the kind of acting common to both sexes. What she wants is to give expression to her own soul, her own womanly nature, the individual emotions of her own physical and psychical being; and she can only accomplish that by being entirely herself, *i.e.*, perfectly natural. That is why she makes gesticulations, and speaks in a tone of voice which is never used elsewhere upon the stage; and she never tries to disguise her age, because her body is nothing more to her than an instrument for expressing her woman's soul.

What is genius? The word has hitherto been understood to imply a superabundance of intelligence, imagination, and passion, combined with a higher order of intellect than that possessed by average persons. Genius was a masculine attribute, and when people spoke of woman's genius, their meaning was almost identical. A finer spiritual susceptibility scarcely came under the heading of genius; it was therefore, upon the whole, a very unsatisfactory definition. There can be no doubt that there is a kind of genius peculiar to women, and it is when a woman is a genius that she is most unlike man, and most womanly; it is then that she creates through the instrumentality of her womanly nature and refined senses. This is the kind of productive faculty which Eleonora Duse possesses to such a high degree.

A woman's productive faculty has always shown a decided preference for authorship and acting,—the two forms of art which offer the best opportunity for the manifestation of the inner life, as being the most direct and spontaneous, and in which there are the fewest technical difficulties to overcome. A woman's impulses are of such short duration that she feels the need for constant change of emotion. The majority of women are attracted by the stage, and there is no form of artistic production which they find more difficult to renounce. Why is this? We will leave vanity and other minor considerations out of the question, and imagine Duse shedding real tears upon the stage, enduring real mental and maybe physical sufferings, experiencing real sorrow and real joy.

And now, putting aside all question of nerves and auto-suggestion, we would ask what it is that attracts a woman to the stage?

Sensation.

A productive nature cannot endure the monotony of real life. To it, real life means uniformity. Uniformity in love, uniformity in work, uniformity in pleasures, uniformity in sorrows. To break through this uniformity—this half sleep of daily existence—is a craving felt by all persons possessed of superfluous vitality. This vitality may be more or less centered on the ego, and for such,—*i.e.*, the persons who are possessed of the largest share of individual, productive vitality,—authorship and acting are the two shortest ways of escape from the uniformity of daily life. Of these two, the last-named form of artistic expression is best suited to woman, and the woman who has felt these sensations, especially the tragic ones, can never tear herself away from the stage. For she experiences them with an intensity of feeling which belongs only to the rarest moments in real life, and which cannot then be consciously enjoyed. But the artificial emotions, which can scarcely be reckoned artificial, since they cause her excited nerves to quiver,—of these she is strangely conscious in her enjoyment of them; she enjoys both spiritual and physical horror, she enjoys the thousand reflex emotions, and she also enjoys the genuine fatigue and bodily weakness which follow after. For the majority of women our life is an everlasting, half-waking expectation of something that never comes, or it may be nothing more than a hard day's work; but life for a talented actress becomes a double existence, filled with warm colors—sorrow and gladness. She can do what other women never can or would allow themselves to do, she can express every sensation that she feels, she can enjoy the full extent of a woman's feelings, and live them over and over again. But because this life is half reality and half fiction, and because the strain of acting is always followed by a feeling of emptiness and dissatisfaction, great actresses are always disillusioned, and that is perhaps the reason why Duse's attractive face wears an expression of weariness and hopeless longing. But the warm colors—the colors of sorrow and passion—are always enticing, and that is why great tragedians can never forsake the stage, although gradually, little by little, the intensity of their feelings grows less, and the colors become pale and more false.

The Woman Naturalist

1

It is a well-known peculiarity of Norwegian authors that they all want something. It is either some of the "new devilries" with which Father Ibsen amuses himself in his old age, or else it is the Universal Disarm-ment Act and the peace of Europe, which Björnson, with his increasing years and increasing folly, assures us will come to pass as a result of "universal morality;" or else it is the rights of the flesh, which have been discovered by Hans Jaeger; but whatever they want, it is always something that has no connection with their art as authors. All their writings assume the form of a polemical or critical discussion on social subjects; yet in spite of their boasted psychology, they care little for the great mystery which humanity offers to them in the un-explored regions lying between the two poles: man and woman; and as for physiology, they are as little concerned about it as Paul Bourget in his *Physiologie de l'Amour Moderne*, where there is no more physiology than there is in the novels of Dumas *père*.

"When the green tree," etc. That is the style of the Norwegian authors; and as for the authoresses of the three Scandinavian coun-tries,—they are all ladies who have been educated in the high schools. They cast down their eyes, not out of shyness,—for the modern woman is too well aware of her own importance to be shy,—but in order to read. They read about life, as it is and as it should be, and then they set themselves down to write about life as it is and as it should be; but they really know nothing of it beyond the little that they see during their afternoon walks through the best streets in the town, and at the evening parties given by the best *bourgeois* society.

This is the case with all Scandinavian authoresses, with one exception. This one exception can see, and she looks at life with good large eyes, opened wide like a child's, and sees with the impartiality that belongs to a healthy nature; she can grasp what she sees, and describe it too, with a freshness and expressiveness which betray a lack of "cultured" reading.

2

A lady of remarkable and brilliant beauty may sometimes be seen in the theatre at Copenhagen, or walking in the streets by the side of a tall, stout, fair gentleman, whose features resemble those of Gustavus Adolphus. Any one can see that the lady is a native of Bergen. To us strangers, the natives of Bergen have a certain something whereby we always recognize them, no matter whether we meet them in Paris or in Copenhagen. Björnson's wife has it as decidedly as the humblest clerk whom we see on Sundays at the table of his employer at Reval or Riga. Their short, straight noses lack earnestness, their hair is shiny and untidy, their eyes are black as pitch, and they have the free and easy movements that are peculiar to a well-proportioned body; it is as though the essence of the vitality of Europe had collected in the old Hanseatic town of the North. I do not think that the inhabitants of Bergen are remarkable for their superior intelligence; if they were it might hinder them from grasping things as resolutely, and dispatching them as promptly as they are in the habit of doing. But among Norwegians, who are known to have heavy, meditative natures, the people of Bergen are the most cheerful and light-hearted,—in as far as it is possible to be cheerful and light-hearted in this world.

The lady who is walking by the side of the man with the Gustavus-Adolphus head is a striking phenomenon in Copenhagen. She is different from every one else, which a lady ought never to be. Compared with the flat-breasted, lively, and flirtatious women of Copenhagen, she, with her well-developed figure and large hips, is like a great sailing-ship among small coquettish pleasure boats. She is always doing something which no lady would do; she wears bright colors, which are not the fashion; and I saw her one evening at an entertainment, where there were not enough chairs, sitting on a table and dangling her feet,—although she is the mother of two grown-up sons!

3

When the woman's rights movement made its appearance in Norway, authoresses sprang up as numerous as mushrooms after the rain. Women claimed the right to study, to plead, and to legislate in the local body and the state; they claimed the suffrage, the right of property, and the right to earn their own living; but there was one very simple right to which they laid no claim, and that was the woman's right to love. To a great extent this right had been thrust aside by the modern social order, yet there were plenty of Scandinavian authors who claimed it; it was only amongst the lady writers that it was ignored. They did not want to risk anything in the company of man; they did not want any love on the fourth story with self-cooked meals; they preferred to criticize man and all connected with him; and they wrote books about the hard-working woman and the more or less contemptible man. The two sexes were a vanquished standpoint. These were completed by the addition of beings who were neither men nor women, and, in consequence of the law of adaptability, they continued to improve with time, and woman became a thinking, working, neutral organism.

Good heavens! When women think!

Among the group of celebrated women-thinkers,—Leffler, Ahlgren, Agrell, etc.,—who criticized love as though it were a product of the intelligence, followed by a crowd of maidenly amazons, there suddenly appeared an author named Amalie Skram, whom one really could not accuse of being too thoughtful. It is true that in her first book there was the intellectual woman and the sensual man, and a seduced servant girl, grouped upon the chessboard of moral discussion with a measured proportion of light and shade,—that was the usual method of treating the deepest and most complicated moments of human life. But this book contained something else, which no Scandinavian authoress had ever produced before: her characters came and went, each in his own way; every one spoke his own language and had his own thoughts; there was no need for inky fingers to point the way; life lived itself, and the horizon was wide with plenty of fresh air and blue sky,—there was nothing cramped about it, like the wretched little extract of life to which the other ladies confined themselves. There was a wealth of minute observation about this book, brought to life by careful painting and critical descriptions, a trustworthy memory and an untroubled honesty; one recognized true naturalism below the hard surface of a problem novel, and one felt that if her talent grew upon the sunny side, the North would gain its first woman naturalist who did not write about life in a critical, moralizing, and polemical manner, but in whom life would reveal itself as bad and as stupid, as full of unnecessary anxiety and unconscious cruelty, as easy-going, as much frittered away and led by the senses as it actually is.

Two years passed by and "Constance Ring," the story of a woman who was misunderstood, was followed by "Sjur Gabriel," the story of a starving west coast fisherman. There is not a single false note in the book, and not one awkward description or superfluous word. It resembles one of those sharp-cut bronze medallions of the Renaissance, wherein the intention of the artist is executed with a perfected technical power in the use of the material. This perfection was the result of an intimate knowledge of the material, and that was Fru Skram's secret. Her soul was sufficiently uncultured, and her sense of harmony spontaneous enough to enable her to reproduce the simplest cause in the heart's fiber. She describes human beings as they are to be found alone with nature,—with a raw, niggardly, unreliable, Northern nature; she tells of their never-ending, unfruitful toil, whether field labor or child-bearing, the stimulating effect of brandy, the enervating influence of their fear of a harsh God,—the God of a severe climate,—the shy, unspoken love of the father, and the overworked woman who grows to resemble an animal more and more. Such are the contents of this simplest of all books, which is so intense in its absolute straightforwardness. The story is told in the severest style, in few words without reflections, but with a real honesty which looks facts straight in the face with unterrified gaze, and is filled with a knowledge of life and of people combined with a breadth of experience which is generally the property of men, and not many men. We are forced to ask ourselves where a woman can have obtained such knowledge, and we wonder how this unconventional mode of thinking can have found its way into the tight-laced body and soul of a woman.

A second book appeared the same year, called "Two Friends." It is the story of a sailing vessel of the same name, which travels backwards and forwards between Bergen and Jamaica, and Sjur Gabriel's grandson is the cabin boy on board. This book offers such a truthful representation of the life, tone of conversation, and work on board a Norwegian sailing vessel, that it would do credit to an old sea captain. The tone is true, the characters are life-like, and the humor which pervades the whole is thoroughly seamanlike. The description of how the entire crew, including the captain, land at Kingston one hot summer night to sacrifice to the Black Venus, and the description of the storm, and the shipwreck of the "Two Friends" on the Atlantic Ocean, the gradual destruction of the ship, the state of mind of the crew, and the captain's suddenly awakened piety;—it is all so perfectly life-like, so characteristically true of the sailor class, and so full of local Norwegian coloring, that we ask ourselves how a woman ever came to write it,—not only to experience it, but to describe it at all, describe as she does with such masterly confidence and such plain expressions, without any affectation, prudery, or conceit, and without any trace of that dilettantism of style and subject which has hitherto been regarded as inseparable from the writings of Scandinavian women.

4

Whence comes this sudden change from the dilettante book, "Constance Ring," with its Björnson-like reflections, to the matured style of "Sjur Gabriel" and "Two Friends"?

I could not understand it all at first, but the day came when I understood. Amalie Skram as a woman and an author had come on to the sunny side.

I have often wondered why it is that so few people come on to the sunny side. I have studied life until I became the avowed enemy of all superficial pessimism and superficial naturalism. I have discovered a secret attraction between happiness and individualism,—an attraction deeper than Zola is able to apprehend; it is the complete human beings who, with wide-opened tentacles, are able to appropriate to their own use everything that their inmost being has need of; but whether a person is or is not a complete human being, that fate decides for them before they are born.

Fru Amalie Skram was, in her way, one of these complete women. She passed unscathed through a girl's education, was perhaps scarcely influenced by it, and with sparkling eyes and glowing cheeks she gazed upon the world and society with the look of a barbaric Northern woman, who retains the full use of her instinct. When quite young she married the captain of a ship, by whom she had two sons. She went with him on a long sea voyage round the world; she saw the Black Sea, the Sea of Azof, and the shores of the Pacific and Atlantic oceans. She saw life on board ship, and life on land,—man's life. Her mind was like a photographic plate that preserves the impressions received until they are needed; and when she reproduced them, they were as fresh and complete as at the moment when they were first taken. These impressions were not the smallware of a lady's drawing-room; they represented the wide horizon, the rough ocean of life with its many dangers. It was the kind of life that brings with it freedom from all prejudice, the kind of life which is no longer found on board a modern steamer going to and fro between certain places at certain intervals.

But it was not to be expected that the monotony of the life could satisfy her. She separated herself from her husband, and remained on shore, where she became interested in various social problems, and wrote "Constance Ring."

It was then that she made the acquaintance of Erik Skram.

The man with the head of Gustavus Adolphus is Denmark's most Danish critic. His name is little known elsewhere, and he cannot be said to have a very great reputation; but this may be partly accounted for by the fact that he has no ambition, and partly because he has one of those profound natures that are rendered passive by the depth of their intellect. He is a man of one book, a novel called "Gertrude Colbjörnson," and he is never likely to write another. But he contributes to newspapers and periodicals, where his spontaneous talent is accompanied by that quiet, delicate, easy-going style which is one of the forms of expression peculiar to the Danish sceptics.

Fru Amalie Müller became Fru Amalie Skram, and the bold Bergen woman, who was likewise the dissatisfied lady reformer of Christiania, became the wife of a born critic, and went to live at Copenhagen. She was an excitable little *brunette*, he a fair, phlegmatic man, and together they entered upon the struggle for the mastery, which marriage always is.

In this struggle Fru Amalie Skram was beaten; every year she became more of an artist, more natural, more simple, more herself, and more of all that a woman never can become when she is left to herself. Her husband's superior culture liberated her fresh, wild, primitive nature from the parasites of social problems; the experienced critic saw that her strength lay in her keen observation, her happy incapacity for reasoning and moralizing, her infallible memory for the impressions of the senses and emotions, and her good spirits, which are nothing more than the result of physical health. He cautiously pushed her into the direction to which she is best suited, to the naturalism which is natural to her. Her books were no longer drawn out, neither were they as poor in substance as books by women generally are, even the best of them; they grew to be more laconic than the majority of men's books, but clear and vivid; there was nothing in them to betray the woman. And after he had done this much for her, the experienced man did yet one thing more,—he gave her the courage of her recollections.

5

Amalie Skram's talent culminated in "Lucie." In this book we see her going about in an untidy, dirty, ill-fitting morning gown, and she is perfectly at home. It would scandalize any lady. Authoresses who struggle fearlessly after honest realism—like Frau von Ebner-Eschenbach and George Eliot—might perhaps have touched upon it, but with very little real knowledge of the subject. Amalie Skram, on the other hand, is perfectly at home in this dangerous borderland. She is much better informed than Heinz Tovote, for instance, and he is a poet who sings of women who are not to be met with in drawing-rooms. She describes the pretty ballet girl with genuine enjoyment and true sympathy; but the book falls into two halves, one of which has succeeded and the other failed. Everything that concerns Lucie is a success, including the part about the fine, rather weak-kneed gentleman who supports her, and ends by marrying her, although his love is not of the kind that can be called "ennobling." All that does not concern Lucie and her natural surroundings is a failure, especially the fine gentleman's social circle, into which Lucie enters after her marriage, and where she seems to be as little at home as Amalie Skram herself. Many an author and epicurean would have hesitated before writing such a book as "Lucie." But Amalie Skram's naturalism is of such an honest and happy nature that any secondary considerations would not be likely to enter her mind, and in the last chapter the brutal naturalism of the story reaches its highest pitch. In the whole of Europe there are only two genuine and honest naturalists, and they are Emile Zola and Amalie Skram.

Her later books—take, for instance, her great Bergen novel, "S. G. Myre," "Love in North and South," "Betrayed," etc.—are not to be compared with the three that we have mentioned. They are naturalistic, of course; their naturalism is of the best kind; they are still *unco in de la nature*, but they are no longer entirely *vu à travers un tempérament*. They are no longer quite Amalie Skram.

Norwegian naturalism—we might almost say Teutonic naturalism—culminated in Amalie Skram, this off-shoot of the Gallic race. Compared with her, Fru Leffler and Fru Ahlgren are good little girls, in their best Sunday pinafores; Frau von Ebner is a maiden aunt, and George Eliot a moralizing old maid. All these women came of what is called "good family," and had been trained from their earliest infancy to live as became their position. All the other women whom I have sketched in this book belonged to the upper classes, and like all women of their class, they only saw one little side of life, and therefore their contribution to literature is worthless as long as it tries to be objective. Naturalism is the form of artistic expression best suited to the lower classes, and to persons of primitive culture, who do not feel strong enough to eliminate the outside world, but reflect it as water reflects an image. They feel themselves in sympathy with their surroundings, but they have not the refined instincts and awakened antipathies which belong to isolation. Where the character differs from the individual consciousness, they do not think of sacrificing their soul as a highway for the multitude, any more than their body—*à la* Lucie—to the *commune bonum*.

A Young Girl's Tragedy

1

It seldom happens that a genuine confession penetrates through the intense loneliness in which a person's inner life is lived; with women, hardly ever. It is rare when a woman leaves any written record of her life at all, and still more rare when her record is of any psychological interest; it is generally better calculated to lead one astray. A woman is not like a man, who writes about himself from a desire to understand himself. Even celebrated women, who are scarce, and candid women, who are perhaps scarcer still, have no particular desire to understand themselves. In fact, I have never known a woman who did not wish, either from a good or bad motive, to remain a *terra incognita* to her own self, if only to preserve the instinctive element in her actions, which might otherwise have perished. There is also another reason for this reticence. A woman does not live the inner life to anything like the same extent as a man; her instincts, occupations, needs, and interests lie outside herself; whereas a man is more self-contained,—his entire being is developed from within. Woman is spiritually and mentally an empty vessel, which must be replenished by man. She knows nothing about herself, or about man, or about the great silent inflexibility of life, until it is revealed to her consciousness by man. But the woman of our time

—and many of the best women, too—manifests a desire to dispense with man altogether; and she whom Nature has destined to be a vessel out of which substance shall grow, wishes to be a substance in herself, out of which nothing can grow, because the substance wherewith she endeavors to fill the void is unorganical, rational, and foreign to her nature. The mistake is tragic, but there is nothing impressive about it; it is merely hopeless, chaotic, heart-rending; and because it is chaotic in itself, it creates a void for the woman who falls into it,—a void in which she perishes. The more talented she is, and the more womanly, the worse it will be for her. And yet it is generally the talented woman who is most strongly attracted by it, and man remains to her both inwardly and outwardly as much a stranger as though he were a being from another planet. What can be the origin of this devastating principle at the core of woman's being? Among all the learned and celebrated women whom I have attempted to depict in this book, there is not one in whom it has not shown itself, either in a lasting or spasmodic form; but neither is there one who did not suffer acutely on account of it. How did it begin in these women, who were so richly endowed, whose natures were so productive? Was it developed by means of outward suggestion? Or does it mark a state of transition between old and new? It is possible that it is not found only amongst women, but that there is something corresponding to it in men. I shall return to this subject afterwards.

Of all the books which women have written about themselves, I only know of two that are written with the unalloyed freshness of spontaneity, and which are therefore genuine to a degree that would be otherwise impossible; these are Mrs. Carlyle's diary and Marie Bashkirtseff's journal. The contents of both books consist chiefly of the cries of despair which issue from the mouths of two women who feel themselves captured and ill-used, and are consequently tired of life, though they do not know the reason nor who is to blame. Mrs. Carlyle was an imbittered woman, unwilling to complain of, yet always indirectly abusing, that disagreeable oddity, Thomas Carlyle; he was an egotistical boor, who required everything and gave nothing in return, and was certainly not the right husband for her. The two books stand side by side: one is the writing of a discontented woman of a much older generation, whose long-suppressed wrath, annoyance, and indignation, combined with bodily and spiritual thirst, resulted in a nervous disease; while the other is far more extraordinary and difficult to comprehend, as it is the writing of a young girl who is rich, talented, and pretty, and who belongs entirely to the present generation of women, since she would be only thirty-four years of age were she living now. Both books are confessions *d'outre tombe*, and they are both the result of a desire to be silent,—a desire not often felt by women.

Mrs. Carlyle maintained this silence all her life long towards her husband, and it was not until after her death that he discovered, by means of the diary, how little he had succeeded in making her happy; his surprise was great. Marie Bashkirtseff also maintained silence towards an all too affectionate family, consisting of women only. They both possessed a strength of mind which is rare in women, and it was owing to this that they did not confide their troubles to any one; theirs was the pride that belongs to solitude, for they had neither women friends nor confidants, and it was only when they were no longer able to contain themselves that some of their best and worst feelings overflowed into these books,—in Mrs. Carlyle's case in a few bittersweet drops, but with Marie Bashkirtseff they were more like a foaming torrent filled with thundering whirlpools, with here and there a few quiet places where the stream widens out into a beautiful clear lake, and thin willows bend over the still waters. The one felt that she had not developed into a full-grown woman by her marriage; the other was a young girl who never grew to be a woman; but both are less interesting on account of what they tell us than on account of that which they have not known how to tell. Marie Bashkirtseff's book, which in the course of ten years has run through almost as many editions, is especially interesting in the latter respect, and is a perfect gold mine for all that has to do with the psychology of young girls.

2

Marie Bashkirtseff was descended from one of those well-guarded sections of society from whence nearly all the women have sprung who have taken any active part in the movements of their time during the latter half of our century. Hers was more than ordinarily happily situated. The two families from whose union she sprang, the Bashkirtseffs and Babanins, were both branches of old South-Russian nobility; but for some reason or other, which she appears never to have ascertained, the marriage between her parents was an unhappy one. They separated after having been married for a couple of years, during which time two children, a son and a daughter, were born, and her mother returned to her old home, accompanied by little Marie. Petted and spoiled by her grandparents, her mother, her aunt, and the governesses, who, even at that early age, were greatly impressed by her numerous talents and determined will, she spent the first years of her life on her grandparents' property; but in May, 1870, the whole family went abroad, including the mother, aunt, grandfather, Marie, her brother, her little cousin, a family doctor, and a large retinue of servants.

For two years they wandered from place to place, staying at Vienna, Baden-Baden, Geneva, and Paris, and finally settling at Nice. It was there that Marie, who was then twelve years of age, began the journal, published after her death at four-and-twenty, which was to be her real life work.

She has bequeathed other tokens of her labor to posterity. They hang in the Luxembourg museum, in the division reserved for pictures by artists of the present day which have been purchased by the State. If we go into one of the smaller side rooms, we are suddenly confronted by a picture of dogs barking in a desert place; there is something so real and vivid about it that the rest of the State-rewarded industry seems pale and lifeless in comparison. A bit of nature in the corner attracts, while it makes us shiver; it is large, bold, brutal,—and what does it represent? Only a couple of street urchins talking to each other as they stand in front of a wooden paling. There is no doubt but that the influence of Bastien Lepage has been at work here. There is something that reminds us of him in the hot, gray, sunless sky; but there is also a certain Russian atmosphere about it that gives a dry look that contrasts strangely with the French landscapes. And where would Bastien Lepage get these contours? We have never seen lines more carelessly drawn, and yet so true; there is real genius in them. This picture is a primitive bit of Russian nature, child-like in its honesty, and the painter is Marie Bashkirtseff.

Near the door hangs a little portrait of a young woman dressed in fur. She has the typical Russian face, with thick, irregular eyebrows, from under which a pair of Tartar eyes look at you straight in the face with a curious expression. What can it be? Is it indifference, or defiance; or is it nothing more than physical well-being?

Among all the pictures painted by women that I have ever seen, I do not remember anywhere the temperament and individuality of the artist are revealed with greater force. The touch is so primitive, so uncultured in the best and worst sense of the word, that it surprises us to think that it is the work of a woman, half child, who belongs to the best society; it would seem rather to suggest the claws of a lioness.

Yet Marie Bashkirtseff was a thorough lady, not only by birth and education, but in her heart as well; she was a lady to the tips of her fingers, to an extreme that was almost absurd; she was not merely a fashionable lady, in the way that certain clever young men take a half ironical pleasure in appearing fashionable, but a lady in real earnest, with all the intensity of a religious bigot.

She had been educated by ladies, by a gentle and refined though rather shallow mother, by an aunt whose vocation seems to have consisted in self-sacrifice for others, a domineering grandmother, two governesses,—one Russian and the other French,—and an "angelical" doctor who lived in the house, and always travelled with them, and who seems to have become somewhat of a woman himself from having lived amongst so many women.

She was no more than twelve years old when she discovered that her governesses were insupportably stupid, and that the only thing that they understood was how to make her waste her precious youth. There was no time for that. She was already aware of the shortness of time, and it was her anxiety to make the most of it that afterwards hurried her short life to its close. She was possessed of an intense thirst for everything,—life, knowledge, enjoyment, sympathy. But although her grandfather had been "Byronic" in his youth, the family passed their lives vegetating with true Russian indolence; there was no help for it; she knew that nothing better was to be expected of them. And accordingly she hunted her governesses out of the house and took her education into her own hands. A tutor was engaged, and a list was made from which no branch of learning was excluded. The tutor nearly fainted with astonishment when it was shown to him, but he was still more astonished at Marie's progress afterwards. Drawing was the only lesson in which the future great artist did not succeed; it bored her, and nothing came of it.

Her inner life, meanwhile, is stirred with tumultuous passions. She is in love, as passionately and as truly in love as any matured woman. And, after all, this thirteen-year-old girl is a matured woman; she is more developed, more truly woman-like than the worn-out woman of three-and-twenty, who only lived with half her strength. The man whom she loves is a very distinguished Englishman, who had bought a villa at Nice, where he spent a few months with his mistress every year,—but this circumstance does not affect Marie in the very least; she is experienced in her knowledge of the world, and by no means bourgeois in her way of thinking. There is another reason, however, that causes her intolerable suffering,—the handsome English duke is too grand for her. She is troubled, not only because he pays her no attention at present, but because she thinks that he is never likely to esteem her sufficiently to wish to marry her, unless, indeed, she could do something to make herself a name, and become celebrated. Marie Bashkirtseff, accordingly, wishes to become celebrated. She would like to be a great singer, who is at the same time a great actress; she would like to have the whole world at her feet, including the duke, and be able to choose between royal dukes and princes, and then she would choose him. For a couple of years or more she lives upon this dream, studies, reads, cries, and suffers that unnecessary overplus of secret pain and anxiety which usually accompanies the development of richly gifted natures.

She has a lovely voice and great dramatic talent, but the former is not fully developed, and cannot be trained for some years to come. She buys cart-loads of books; but as there is no one to guide her choice, and her social intercourse does not diverge a hairbreadth outside her family and a small circle of friends, consisting chiefly of compatriots, it is only natural that her reading should be confined to Dumas *père*, Balzac, Octave Feuillet, and such literary tallow candles as Ohnet, and others like him. Her taste remains uncultivated, her horizon bounded by the family, and her knowledge continues to be a mixture of ancient superstitions combined with the newest shibboleths.

Her most familiar converse is between herself and her Creator, whom her imagination pictures as a kind of superior great-grandfather, very grand and powerful, and the only One in whom she can confide. To Him she lays bare her heart, beseeching Him to give her that which is a necessity of life to her, and she makes numerous promises, to be fulfilled only on condition that her prayers are granted; she respects what she conceives to be His wishes with regard to prayer and almsgiving, and overwhelms Him with reproaches if these are of no avail. And they are of no avail. Her voice, which has been tried and praised by the highest musical authorities in Paris, is being gradually undermined by a disease of the throat, and the duke marries; thus her hopes of becoming famous and of gaining a great love are gone, gone forever.

Those were the first and second cruel wounds wherewith life made its presence felt in this sensitive soul; they were wounds which never healed, and which imparted hidden veins of venom to the healthy parts of her being.

Does not this remind us of the fairy tale about wounds that never heal? Is not this just the way that the wounds made by Fate, or by human beings, in our souls continue to bleed forever? They are like tender places, which shrink from the touch throughout a lifetime, and wither if a breath passes over them. The more sensitive a person is, the more painful they are, and nothing is so easily wounded as a growing organism. The nerves have a good memory, better even than the brain, and there are some wounds received in youth and impressed during growth which seem to have been wiped out ages ago, till suddenly they present the appearance of a putrefying spot, a poisonous place, the point of disintegration of the entire organism. Or there may be something crippled in the person's vitality. They live on, but one muscle, perhaps only a very small one, is strained and just a little out of order, and the soul is compelled to replace what the body lacks by means of extra exertion, which is afterwards paid for by excessive weariness.

There are some sluggish natures, especially among women, who exert their strength to the least possible degree, and do their work in a half-hearted manner. There are also souls which seem all aglow with the psychic and sensuous warmth of their natures, who carry the whole substance of their being in the hand, and who give themselves up entirely to the interest of what they are feeling and wishing for at the moment. Their path is strewn with fragments of their life, which fall off dead, and every stroke aimed at them hits the heart. Their soul has no covering to protect them from disappointment; neither have they the forgetful sleep of animals, wherein the body is at rest. But such natures are generally possessed of an endless supply of self-sustaining strength, which imbues them with the power to grow again; and although their wounds are plentiful, their germinating cells are plenteous also. The parts that are crippled remain crippled still, but new possibilities are continually developing in new directions.

The young girl of whose silly, half-fancied love story I have made so much, was one of these natures. She was formed of the material out of which destiny either molds women who become the greatest of their sex, or else casts them aside, discarded and broken. It generally depends upon some very trifling matter which of the two takes place. Marie was an exceedingly spoiled child when the first blow fell; but there was something lacking in her nature—a dead spot that revealed itself with the destruction of her voice—while her body was blossoming into womanhood. There was a dead spot somewhere without as well, something that lacked in life, else it were not possible to long so ardently and not obtain. There was something that gazed at her with evil, ghost-like eyes, causing her nerves to quiver beneath its icy breath. She was a brave girl. She did not complain, did not look back, but drew herself together, silent and determined. Her passionate love of work took the form of painting, and as she could not become a great singer, she meant to be a great painter. But a part of her being congealed and withered away; her young heart had expanded to receive a return of the love it had so freely given, and was left unsatisfied.

The years passed in much the same way as they had passed before for this spoiled child of fortune. A few people who were indifferent to her died, and others came who were no less indifferent. They travelled from Nice to Paris, and from Paris to Nice, but she was equally lonely everywhere. She had no playfellows, no girl friends, no school-room companions, and to life's contrasts she remained a stranger. Her cousin Dina was the only one who was always with her, and she was the typical girl,—a pretty, good-natured nonentity. And thus, though always lonely, she was never alone. Wherever she went, her mother and aunt went with her, and wherever they did not go, Marie Bashkirtseff did not go either. In all her journeyings, she never received a single impression for herself alone; it was always reflected at the same moment in the sunglasses of her aunt and mother, and never a word did she hear but was also heard by her duennas. No man was allowed within the circle of her acquaintance until he had first been judged suitable from a marriageable, as well as a social point of view. The female atmosphere by which she was surrounded paralyzed every other.

It was her destiny!

Life was empty around her, and in the void her excited nerves became even more and more centered upon her own ego. Her opinion of herself assumed gigantic proportions, and whatever there had been of soul grandeur in her nature was changed into admiration of self. And yet, in spite of all, this girl, who was undoubtedly a genius, never realized her own power to the full. The natural nobility of her feelings assumed a moral, bourgeois dress, and her young senses, which had manifested such a passionate craving at their first awakening, withered and grew numb.

She was sixteen when she experienced her second disappointment in love, and it became for her the turning-point of her inner life.

At her earnest request the family had gone to Rome. It was the time of the Carnival, and after the conventional life at Nice, the sudden outbreak of merriment in the Eternal City called forth a frivolous mood in every one. There was something delightful in the ease with which acquaintances were made, and the simple, straightforward manner in which homage was done. A young man makes love to Dina; he belongs to an old, aristocratic, Roman family, and is the nephew of an influential cardinal. Marie entices him away from her, and the young Italian falls a prey to the brilliant fascination and wild coquetry of her manner. He is dazzled by such aggressive conduct on the part of so young a girl, and the equivocal character of it spurs him on. He storms her with declarations of love, and Marie reciprocates his passion,—not very seriously perhaps, but her senses, her vanity, her pride, all are on fire. The young man communicates to her something of his habitual good spirits, and her head, no less than the heads of her mother and aunt, is completely turned at the prospect of such a distinguished *parti*. The family set to work in good earnest to bring matters to a climax, for which object they employ suitable deputies, while Marie persistently holds the legitimate joys of marriage before the face of her importunate lover. The Italian slips past these dangerous rocks with the dexterity of an eel. He knows what Marie and the house of Bashkirtseff, convinced as they are of the grandeur of their Russian ancestry, cannot realize,—that for him, the heir and nephew of the cardinal, no marriage will be considered suitable unless it brings with it connection with the nobility, or the advantages of an immense fortune; and in this opinion he fully concurs. The result is that they are always at cross purposes: he talks of love, she of marriage; he of *tête-à-têtes* on the staircase after midnight, she of betrothal kisses between lunch and dinner under the auspices of her family. When his allusions to his uncle's disapproval of a marriage with a heretical Russian lady from the provinces do not produce any effect on the family other than indignation, expressive of their wounded feelings, he goes away, and allows himself to be sent into retreat in a monastery. While there, he ascertains that the Bashkirtseffs have left Rome and given up all desire to have such a vacillating creature for a son-in-law. They go to Nice, and no more is said about him until Marie persuades her family to return to Rome, where she meets him at a party, but only to discover that he loves her when there, and forgets her again the moment that she is out of sight. This was the second time that she had knocked at the door of life; and, as on the former occasion, Fate held back the joys which she seemed to have in store, only opening the door wide enough to let in the face of a grinning Punchinello.

Few writers have attempted to describe the state of a young girl's mind on such occasions, when a thousand cherished hopes are instantaneously charred as though struck by lightning, and, worse still, all that she had wished for becomes hateful in her eyes, and the shame of it assumes a gigantic scale, and continues to increase, though maybe at the cost of her life. Men have no suspicion of this, and they would find it hard to understand, even supposing that they were given the opportunity of observing it. They grow up amid the realities of life; a girl, in the unreal. The disappointments which a man endures are real ones, and unless he is a fool, he is in a position to form an approximate valuation of his own importance. With a girl it is different; her opinion of herself is exaggerated to an extent that is quite fantastical and altogether unreal, and this is especially the case when her education is of a strictly conventional character, and has been conducted mainly by women. The preservation of her purity is the foundation of her creed, but she is not told, nor does she guess, wherein this purity consists, nor how it may be lost; and consequently she imagines that it can be lost in every conceivable way,—by a mere nothing, by a pressure of the hand, but in any case by a kiss. This kiss Marie Bashkirtseff had actually given and received, and after it she had been forgotten and despised! That kiss branded her in secret all her life. She never forgot it.

This is not the only consequence of the change from the real to the unreal which takes place when the outer world casts its reflection in the mirror of a young girl's soul. Every girl has an exaggerated idea of the value of the mystic purity of her maidenhood in the eyes of men; and when she makes a man happy by the gift of herself, she imagines that she has given him something extraordinary, which he must accept on bended knee. What words can describe the humiliation which she feels if he does not set a sufficiently high value on the gift, or if he thrusts it aside like a pair of old slippers that do not fit! All girls are silly to a certain extent, even the cleverest; and the girl who is not silly on this point must have lost something of her girlish modesty.

In the case of Marie Bashkirtseff, a part of her being was blighted after her encounter with the Italian, and she never entirely recovered from the effects of it. This, her first acquaintance with a man, was so full of racial misunderstandings and others besides, that it destroyed her faith in man, as indeed it is doomed to be destroyed sooner or later in every girl with a strong individuality and healthy nature. And for her, as for many another, followed the lifeless years into the middle of the twenties, when a new and very different faith begins to show itself as the result of wider views of life and internal changes. But with her this faith never came. Her vitality gave way too soon. Those dead years which must inevitably follow upon an all too promising and too early maturity, leaving a young woman apparently trivial and devoid of any true individuality of character, and which often last until the thirties, when the time comes for a new and greater change,—those years with Marie, as with many another "struggling" girl, were filled with an unnatural craving for work.

She wanted to be something on her own account, as an individual. She compelled her mother and aunt to go with her to Paris, where she could go to Julian's studio, which was the only one for women where painting was taught seriously. The working hours were from eight to twelve, from one to five.

But she worked longer. This spoiled child, who had never known what it meant to exert herself, was not satisfied with eight hours of hard labor. She works in the evenings as well, after she comes home; she works on Sundays; she is dead to the world, and with the exception of her daily bath, she renounces every luxury of the toilet, and succeeds in condensing into two years the work of seven. One day Julian tells her that she must work alone, "because," he says, "you have learned all that it is possible to teach."

3

Marie Bashkirtseff was not born an artist, with that stern predestination with which nature determines the career of persons with one talent. If her voice had not been destroyed during its development, she would in all probability have become one of those great singers whose charm lies not only in the outward voice, but in the indescribable fascination of a deep, strong individuality. Her journal, especially the first part, reveals an authoress with a rare psychological intuition, an understanding of human nature, a deep sympathy, a mastery of expression, and an early-matured genius, which are unsurpassed even among Russians, well known for the richness of their temperament. If this young woman, whose short life was consumed by a craving for love, had gained the experience she so greatly desired, where would the woman be found who could have borne comparison with her? Who like her was created to receive the knowledge whereby a woman is first revealed to herself, and is developed into the being who is earth's ruler,—the great mother, on whose lap man reposes, and from whence he goes forth into the world? All that she had was original; it was all of the best material that the earth has to give; and therein lay the mystery of her downfall.

The backbone of her nature was that indomitable pride whereby a great character reveals the consciousness of its own importance. The lioness cannot wed with the house-dog. The same instinct which, in animals, marks the boundary line between the different species, determines in a still higher degree—higher far than the materialistic wisdom of our schools will allow—the attractions and antipathies of love. The iron law which compels healthy natures to preserve their distinction, prevented this girl from sinking to the level of the men of her own class, amongst whom she might have found some to love her. She tried it more than once, but it did not answer. Her exceptionable nature required a husband superior to herself. One or two such men might be found nowadays, who not only as productive minds, but also in the subtle charm of their manly characters, would have been the born masters of an enchantress such as Marie Bashkirtseff. But these men are not to be met with in the drawing-rooms and studios of Paris, nor yet in the Bois de Boulogne; not in St. Petersburg either, nor on the family estates of Little Russia, and she never got to know them.

This woman, who was born to become a great singer, a great painter, a great writer, born—before all else—to be loved with a great love, never learned to know love, and died without being great in any way, because she was enchained all her life long to that which was greater than all her possibilities,—a young girl's infinite ignorance.

In spite of all the knowledge that she had acquired, in spite of all the probings of her sensitive nerves and sharp intellect, she remained always and in everything incomplete. It is one of the results of the incompleteness of which unmarried women are the victims, that they seek everywhere the complete, the perfected in man,—*i.e.*, they seek for that which is only to be found in men who are growing old, and have nothing more to give; in whom there are no slumbering ambitions, and no hidden aspirations. She must have passed by, unheeding, many a young genius, who perhaps went to an inferior woman to satisfy the passion which might have proved to both of them an endless source of blessedness, health, and regeneration. She must have felt many a look rest upon her, arousing sensations which, to her white soul, were a mystery. For this girl, who had drunk deeply of the literature of her time, and who knew theoretically everything that there was to know, was yet unspoiled by a single trace of premature knowledge. The pages of her journal are innocent from beginning to end,—an innocence that is stupid while it is touchingly intact. Marie Bashkirtseff's journal is not merely a contribution to the psychology of girls, it is a young girl's psychology in the widest, most typical sense,—the psychology of the unmarried state, bequeathed by one who is ignorant to those who know, as her only memorial upon earth, but a memorial that will last longer than marble or bronze. She died young, but she had no wish to die. She took twelve years to write this book, and she wrote it on her travels, in the midst of her pleasures, in the midst of her work, in the despair of her loneliness, and in her fear when she shrank from death; she wrote it during sleepless nights, and on days passed in blessed abstraction in the beauties of nature. She always addressed the unknown hearers who were ever present to her imagination; she spoke to them so that, in case she should die young, she might live upon earth in the memory of the strangers who happened to read her journal. A "human document," by a young girl, she thought, must be of sufficient interest not to be forgotten, and she promises to tell us everything connected with her little person. "All, all,—not only all her thoughts, but she will not even hide what is laughable and disadvantageous to herself; for what would be the object of a book like this, unless it told the truth absolutely, accurately, and without concealment?"

The confessions are by no means a human document in the sense that her three patron saints—Zola, Maupassant, and Goncourt—would have used the word. They do not contain a single naked reality. They are modest, not only with the modesty of a child of nature, but with the modesty of a young hot-house beauty, a delicate lady of fashion, beneath whose snow-white resplendent dress—the work of a Parisian dressmaker—are concealed the bleeding wounds and the pitiless signs of death. But she lets us follow her from the rich beginnings of her youth onwards, until the stream of life trickles away drop by drop, leading us on to the weary resignation of her last days.

This exhaustion begins to show itself immediately after the two years of reckless overwork and study in Julian's studio; but the cause of it was mental rather than physical. Julian's last words were: "You have learned all that it is possible to teach—the rest depends upon yourself." And Robert-Fleury, the principal academical professor, nodded his approval. After that they left her. But where was she to begin? Where was the rest to come from? What was she to do—she, who had been such a phenomenal pupil? How was she to obtain sufficient individuality for original production? Learn! yes, of course. A girl can do that better than the most painstaking young man of the faculty. There is nothing to prevent it; her sex will slumber as long as the brain is kept at work. But artistic production is another matter. Whence should it come? Not from herself, for she has nothing; she has had no experience. She can represent what she has seen, or she can imagine, but that is all. Marie's nature was too truthful to be satisfied with imitation. The old academical art did not appeal to her, as was very natural, and the new was just bursting its shell, and contained all the impurity and rubbish that belongs to a state of transition. The imperfect in her desired the perfect; she who was an incomplete woman felt the need of a perfected man.

She made no progress She painted at home from models, and she went out driving with her maid, accompanied by some young Russian friends, and sketched street scenes from the carriage. So great was her need for ideas that she attempted pictures on religious and historical subjects, and with some difficulty she finished a picture for the next Salon,—went half mad with empty pride, but had to admit that it was very much inferior to the former one which she had painted under Julian's supervision. For two years she meets with no success. Her pictures contain nothing that is characteristic; she has no individual style, no personal experiences, and no original ideas. But her individuality, though dormant, is too strong to allow her to imitate the style of other lady artists, one half of whom are too amateurish, and their painting too devoid of character, to content her, while the others have betrayed their sex, and adopted a severe, masculine style.

At last the day came when Bastien Lepage was a public celebrity. Marie Bashkirtseff saw his pictures, became his pupil, worshipped him, and ever after sang his praises.

Yet, in all this, there was something lacking.

His bright coloring, and the atmosphere of his landscapes, with their pale, sultry heat, the aggressive physical character of his people, etc.,—all these points appealed strongly to her South-Russian nature. He set free her national feelings, which had hitherto been bound and suppressed beneath academical influences, and she discovered a kindred spirit in him, a primitive element at the root of his being, which made her tenderly disposed towards him. But she had no intention of remaining his pupil. She was too deeply conscious of the difference between them, and saw clearly that his influence was not likely to be more than a passing phase.

She worshipped him from a long-suppressed desire to worship some one, but her worship was calm and passionless. This little Bastien Lepage was not the man to arouse her deepest affections; he was too bourgeois, and his fine art was too tame.

And yet she praised him, half mechanically. Saint Marceaux, the sculptor, had appealed to her feelings more deeply than he had done.

There was a reason for it. There was a strong tie between these two beings, who seemed only destined to exert a passing influence over one another.

They were both ill when they made each other's acquaintance: life, with its deceptive pleasures, had ruined the health of Bastien Lepage; and Marie Bashkirtseff was ill from want of life,—her youth, her beauty, her vitality, had all been wasted.

It is the usual fate of the cultured young people of our time: he comes to her ruined, because he has satiated his thirst; she comes to him ruined, because her thirst has never been satisfied.

They are as far apart as two separate worlds, and they do not understand one another.

The development of the last few years, through which Marie Bashkirtseff had passed before she met Bastien Lepage, had brought her and the readers of her journal nothing but pain and dulness.

What with ambitious plans for artistic work, and the life with her family,—which resembled a convent more than anything else, interrupted by occasional smart dinners, balls, and various projects of worldly marriages, which came to nothing,—Marie Bashkirtseff had become superficial and almost stupid. Her genius appeared to have flown, and a sickly, *blasée* hot-house plant, solely occupied with herself, was all that remained of her. She was like the ordinary girl of good family, who has grown rather disagreeable, and is no longer quite young, who is still ignorant of most things, and becomes extremely tiresome by chattering on subjects which she does not understand. All this is changed after her meeting with Bastien Lepage.

She regains her youth in a wonderful way; she becomes shy and easily bewildered. When he pays his first visit she gets quite confused, turns back three times before entering the drawing-room, and cannot think of anything to say after they have shaken hands. But he, with his unaffected manner, and little insignificant person, soon succeeds in putting her at her ease. The long tirades in her journal come to an end at last, and are followed by short, cautious, but very expressive sentences.

Bastien Lepage is anything but a lover. His manner is straightforward and simple, and he holds himself strikingly aloof, maybe for want of practice in the art of love-making, or perhaps out of sheer weariness.

When he leaves her, she becomes as vain and egotistical as before; but when he is there she watches his every movement with a still, calm joy.

She had been ill for several years. One lung was affected, and now the other followed suit; she also suffered from deafness, and that troubled her more than anything else. She had never given a thought to her health.

When Bastien is there, all is well. She is always able to hear what he says, and in his eyes she is always pretty; her art takes a new turn, and inspired by him she becomes original. The result is the picture in the Luxembourg, called "A Meeting," besides several very good portraits. There is no question of love between them; he is never anything but the artist, and her old coquettish manner vanishes. She has a peculiarly tender affection for him, and the development from a self-centered girl to a full-grown woman is accomplished within her.

He suddenly becomes violently and hopelessly ill. He is seized with violent pains, followed by the cramp, and his legs are paralyzed.

The green bud of her love withers without ever having blossomed. But as his illness grows worse, his longing to have Marie always beside him increases. When he is sufficiently free from pain to go out driving, he gets his brother to carry him up to her; and at other times she comes with her mother to visit him. It is quite a little idyl. His mother, a worthy woman of the working-class, cooks his soup; while her mother, who is a smart lady, cuts his hair, which has grown too long, and his brother, the architect, crops his beard. After their united efforts he looks as handsome as ever, and no longer so ill. Then Marie must sit by his bedside, while he turns his back upon the others and looks only at her,—and speaks of art.

It is September, 1884. Marie coughs and coughs. Bastien is getting worse and worse, and he cannot bear her to leave him, even while he is undergoing his worst paroxysms of pain. On the 1st of October she writes in her journal:

"*Tant de dégoût et tant de tristesse!*

"What is the use of writing?

"Bastien Lepage is getting worse and worse.

"And I cannot work.

"My picture will not be finished.

"Alas! Alas!

"He is dying and suffers a great deal. When one is with him, one seems to have left the world behind. He is already beyond our reach, and there are days when the same feeling comes over me. I see people, they talk, and I answer; but I seem to be no longer on the earth,—a quiet indifference, not painful, almost like an opium dream. And he is dying! I go there more from habit than anything else; he is a shadow of his former self, and I, too, am scarcely more than a shadow; what is the good of it all?

"He is hardly conscious of my presence now; there is little use in going; I have not the power to enliven him. He is contented to see me, and that is all.

"Yes, he is dying, and it is all the same to me; I do not take myself to account for it; it is something that cannot be helped.

"Besides, what difference does it make?

"All is over.

"In 1885 they will bury me."

In that she was mistaken, for she died the same month. Until the last few days Bastien Lepage had himself carried up to her; and she, shaken by the fever of the last stage of consumption, had her bed moved into the drawing-room, where she could receive him. There, by her bed-side, as she had formerly sat beside his, with his legs resting upon a cushion, he remained until the evening. They scarcely spoke; they were together, and that was all they cared for. And she, who ever since her first awakening consciousness had yearned so passionately and so impatiently for permission to live her life, died now, silent, resigned, without a murmur; and knowing that the end was near, she was great in death, since she had not succeeded in being great in her short life.

4

What remained of her? A book of a thousand pages, of which, in ten years, nearly ten thousand copies were sold, which André Theuriet provided with an introductory poem written in his best style, and to which Maurice Barrès dedicated an altar built by himself and sanctified a rather mistaken Marie Bashkirtseff cult. There was also "A Meeting" in the Luxembourg, which, according to Marie Bashkirtseff's own report, Bastien Lepage criticized as follows: "He says that it is comparatively easy to do *choses canailles*, peasants, street urchins, and especially caricatures; but to paint beautiful things, and to paint them with character,—there is the difficulty."

In order to complete the sketch of this girl, in[178] which I have tried especially to accentuate the typical element, I should like to let her speak for herself, with her characteristic expressions, her impulsive views and peculiar temperament.

At the age of thirteen, she writes:—

"My blood boils, I am quite pale, then suddenly the blood rises to my head, my cheeks burn, my heart beats, and I cannot remain quiet anywhere; the tears burn within me, I force them back, and that only makes me more miserable; all this undermines my health, ruins my character, makes me irritable and impatient. One can always see it in a person's face, whether they take life quietly. As for me, I am always excited. When they deprive me of my time for learning, they rob me for the whole of my life. When I am sixteen or seventeen, my mind will be occupied with other thoughts; now is the time to learn."

And afterwards, with a depth of understanding worthy of Nietzsche:—

"All that I say is not original, for I have no originality. I live only outside myself. To walk or to stand still, to have or not to have, it is all the same to me. My sorrows, my joys, my troubles do not exist...."

And again:—

"I want to live faster, faster, fast.... I am afraid it is true that this longing to live with the speed of steam foretells a short life...."

"Would you believe it? To my mind everything is good and beautiful, even tears, even pain. I like to cry, I like to be in despair, I like to be sad. I like life, in spite of all. I want to live. I long for happiness, and yet I am happy when I am sad. My body cries and shrieks; but something in me, which is above me, enjoys it all."

Then this simile, drawn with wonderful delicacy:—

"At every little sorrow my heart shrinks into itself, not for my own sake, but out of pity—I do not know whether anybody will understand what I mean—every sorrow is like a drop of ink that falls into a glass of water; it cannot be obliterated, it unites itself with its predecessors and makes the clear water gray and dirty. You may add as much water as you like, but nothing will make it clear again. My heart shrinks into itself, because every sorrow leaves a stain on my life, and on my soul, and I watch the stains increasing in number on the white dress which I ought to have kept clean."

At the age of fourteen she wrote these prophetic words:—

"Oh! how impatient I am. My time will come; I believe it, yet something tells me that it will never come, that I shall spend the whole of my life waiting, always waiting. Waiting ... waiting!"

When she was sixteen, at the time of the incident with the cardinal's nephew:—

"If I am as pretty as I think, why is it that no one loves me? People look at me! They fall in love! But they do not love me! And I do so want to be loved."

At seventeen, the first entry in her journal for that year:—

"When shall I get to know what this love is of which we hear so much?"

Later on:—

"Very much disgusted with myself. I hate all that I do, say, and write. I despise myself, because not a single one of my expectations has been fulfilled. I have deceived myself.

"I am stupid, I have no tact, and I never had any. I thought I was intellectual, but I have no taste. I thought I was brave; I am a coward. I believed I had talent, but I do not know how I have proved it."

At the age of eighteen:—

"My body like that of an antique goddess, my hips rather too Spanish, my breast small, perfectly formed, my feet, my hands, my child-like head. *À quoi bon?* When no one loves me.

"There is one thing that is really beautiful, antique: that is a woman's self-effacement in the presence of the man she loves; it must be the greatest, most self-satisfying delight that a superior woman can feel."

In 1882, at the beginning of her illness:—

"So I am consumptive, and have been so for the last two or three years. It is not yet bad enough to die of it.... Let them give me ten years longer, and in these ten years, fame or love, and I shall die contented, at the age of thirty."

The following year:—

"No, I never was in love, and I never shall be any more; a man would have to be very great to please me now, I require so much....

"And simply to fall in love with a handsome boy,—no, it would not answer. Love could no longer wholly occupy me now; it would be a matter of secondary importance, a decoration to the building, an agreeable superfluity. The idea of a picture or a statue keeps me awake for nights together, which the thought of a handsome man has never done."

In another place:—

"Whom shall I ask? Who will be truthful? Who will be just?"

"You, my only friend, you at least will be truthful, for you love me. Yes, I love myself, myself only."

Two weeks before her death, after a visit from Bastien Lepage:—

"I was dressed entirely in lace and plush, all white, but different kinds of white; Bastien Lepage opened his eyes wide with joy.

"'If only I could paint!' he said.

"'And I!'

"Obliged to give it up,—the picture for this year!"

Her portrait represents the face of a typical beauty of Little Russia; the firm, dark eyebrows, arched over eyes that are far apart, give the face an expression that is peculiarly honest and straightforward. The eyes gaze fixedly and dreamily into the distance; the nose is short, with nostrils slightly distended, the mouth soft and determined, with the upper lip passionately compressed. The face is round as a child's, and the neck short and powerful, on a squarely built, fully developed body.

6

The Woman's Rights Woman

1

The latter half of our century is comparatively poor in remarkable women. Nowadays, when women are more exacting than they used to be, they are of less importance than of old. We have rows of women artists, women scientists, and authoresses; the countries of Europe are overrun with them, but they are all mediocrities; and in the upper classes, although there are plenty of eccentric ladies, they are abnormities, not individuals. The secret of a woman's power has always lain in what she is, rather than in what she does, and that is where the women of to-day appear to be strangely lacking. They do all kinds of things, they study and write books without number, they collect money for various objects, they pass examinations and take degrees, they hold meetings and give lectures, they start societies, and there never was a time when women lived a more public life than at present. Yet, with all that, they are of less public importance than they used to be. Where are the women whose drawing-rooms were filled with the greatest thinkers and most distinguished men of their day? They do not exist. Where are the women with delicate tact, who took part in the affairs of the nation? They are a myth. Where are the women whose influence was acknowledged to be greater than the counsel of ministers? Where are the women whose love is immortalized in the works of the greatest poets? Where are the women whose passionate devotion was life and joy to man, bearing him on wings of gladness towards the unknown, and leading him back to the beautiful life on earth? They have been, but where are they now? The more that woman seeks to exert her influence by main force, the less her influence as an individual; the more she imbues this century with her spirit, the fewer her conquests as woman. Her influence on the literature of the eighties has shown itself in an intense, ingrained hatred. It is she who has inspired man to write his hymn of hatred to woman,—Tolstoi in the "Kreutzer Sonata," Strindberg in a whole collection of dramas, Huysman in "En Ménage," while many a lesser star is skeptical of love; and in the writings of the younger authors, where this skepticism is not so apparent, we find that they understand nothing at all about women. It is a peculiar sign of the times that, in spite of the many restrictions of former days, men and women never have stood wider apart than at present, and have never understood one another more badly than now. The honest, unselfish sympathy, the true, I should like to say organical union, which is still to be observed in the married life of old people, seems to have vanished. Each goes his or her own way; there may be a nervous search for each other and a short finding, but it is soon followed by a speedy losing. Is it the men who are to blame? The men of former days were doubtless very different, but in their relations to women they were scarcely more sociable than at present.

Or is it the women who are at fault? For some time past I have watched life in its many phases, and I have come to the conclusion that it is the woman who either develops the man's character or ruins it. His mother, and the woman to whom he unites himself, leave an everlasting mark upon the impressionable side of his nature.

In most cases the final question is not, What is the man like? but, What kind of a woman is she? And I think that the answer is as follows: A woman's actions are more reasonable than they used to be, and her love is also more reasonable. The consequence is a lessening of the passion that is hers to give, which again results in a corresponding coolness on the part of the man. The modern system of educating girls by teaching them numerous languages, besides many other branches of knowledge, encourages a superficial development of the understanding, and renders women more exacting, without making them more attractive; and while the average level of intelligence among women is raised, and the self-conceit of the many largely increased, the few who are original characters will in all probability disappear beneath the pressure of their own sex, and in consequence of the apathy which governs the mutual relations of both sexes.

The age in which we live has produced another class of women in their stead, who, since they represent the strongest majority, must be reckoned as the type. It is natural that they should have neither the influence nor the fascination of the older generation, and they are not as happy. They are neither happy themselves, nor do they make others happy; the reason is that they are less womanly than the others were. From their midst the modern authoresses have gone forth, women who in days to come will be named in connection with the progress of culture; and I think that Anne Charlotte Edgren-Leffler, Duchess of Cajanello, will long be remembered as the most characteristic representative of the type.

2

She was the supporter of a movement that originated with her, and ceased when she died. She was known in countries far beyond her native Sweden; her books were read and discussed all over Germany, and her stories were published in the *Deutsche Rundschau*. She had a clearer brain than most women writers; she could look reality in the face without being afraid, and indeed she was not one who was easily frightened. She was very independent, and understood the literary side of her calling as well as its practical side, and her struggles were by no means confined to her writings She threw aside the old method of seeking to gain her ends by means of womanly charm; she wanted to convince as a woman of intellect. She condemned the old method which used to be considered the special right of women, and fought for the new right, *i.e.*, recognition as a human being. All her arguments were clear and temperate; she was not emotional. The minds from which she fashioned her own were Spencer and Stuart Mill. Nature had endowed her with a proud, straightforward character, and she was entirely free from that affected sentimentality which renders the writings of most women unendurable.

In the course of ten years she became celebrated throughout Europe, and she died suddenly about six months after the birth of her first child. Sonia Kovalevsky, the other and greater European celebrity, who was Professor of Mathematics, and her most intimate friend, also died suddenly, as did several others,—Victoria Benediktson (Ernst Ahlgren), her fellow-countrywoman, and for many years her rival; Adda Ravnkilde, a young Danish writer, who wrote several books under her influence; and a young Finnish authoress named Thedenius. The last three died by their own hands; Sonia Kovalevsky and Fru Edgren-Leffler died after a short illness.

Fru Leffler was the eldest,—she lived to be forty-three; the others died younger,—the last two very much younger. But they all made the same attempt, and they all failed. They wanted to stand alone, they demanded their independence, they tried to carry into practice their views with regard to man.

George Sand made the same attempt, and she succeeded. But then her independence took a very different form from theirs. She followed the traditions of her family, and set no barriers to love; she drank of the great well of life until she had well-nigh exhausted it. She was quite a child of the old *régime* in her manner of life. The efforts made by these other women, at the close of the nineteenth century, took the form of wishing to dispense with man altogether. It is this feature of Teutonic chastity, bounding on asceticism, that was the tragic moment in the lives of all these short-lived women.

It is a strange piece of contemporary history of which I am about to write. It is this that is the cause of the despondent mood peculiar to the last decade of our century; it is this that acts as a weight upon our social life, that makes our leisure wearisome, our joys cold. It is this decay in woman's affection that is the greatest evil of the age.

One of the tendencies of the time is the craving for equality, which seeks to develop woman's judgment by increasing her scientific knowledge. It might have answered from the woman's point of view, so far, at least, as the man was concerned, for it does not much matter to a woman whom she loves, as long as she loves some one. But women have become so sensible nowadays that they refuse to love without a decisive guarantee, and this calculating spirit has already become to them a second nature to so great an extent that they can no longer love, without first taking all kinds of precautionary measures to insure their future peace and comfortable maintenance, to say nothing of the unqualified regard which they expect from their husbands.

All things are possible from a state of mind such as we have described, except love, and love cannot flourish upon it. If there is a thing for which woman is especially created,—that is, unless she happens to be different from other women,—it is love. A woman's life begins and ends in man. It is he who makes a woman of her. It is he who creates in her a new kind of self-respect by making her a mother; it is he who gives her the children whom she loves, and to him she owes their affection. The more highly a woman's mind and body are developed, the less is she able to dispense with man, who is the source of her great happiness or great sorrow, but who, in either case, is the only meaning of her life. For without him she is nothing.

The woman of to-day is quite willing to enjoy the happiness which man brings, but when the reverse is the case, she refuses to submit. She thinks that, with a little precaution, she can bring the whole of life within the compass of a mathematical calculation. But before she has finished her sum, and proved it to see if it is correct, happiness and sorrow have flown past her, leaving her desolate and forsaken,—hardened for want of love, miserable in spite of a cleverly calculated marriage, and imbittered in the midst of joyless ease and sorrow unaccounted for.

Such was the fate of these five short-lived authoresses, although they might not have described it as I have done. Anne Charlotte Edgren-Leffler was chief among the Scandinavian women's rights women who have made for themselves a name in literature. Her opinions were scattered abroad among thousands of women in Germany and in the North, and as she died without being able to dig up the seed which she had sown, she will always be considered as a type of the *fin de siècle* woman, and will remain one of its historical characters.

I write this sketch in the belief that it will not be very unlike the one she would have written of herself, had she lived long enough to do so.

3

Anne Charlotte Leffler was born at Stockholm, and, like all her townsfolk, she was tall, strong, and somewhat angular. She was by nature cold and critical, and in this respect she did not differ from the women of North Sweden. The daughter of a college rector, she had received a thoroughly good education, and was probably far better educated than the majority of women, as she grew up in the companionship of two brothers, who were afterwards professors.

When she was nineteen years of age, she published her first work, a little play, in two acts, called "The Actress." The piece describes the struggle between love and talent, and the scene is laid in the rather narrow sphere of a small country town. The characters are decidedly weak, but not more so than one would naturally expect from the pen of an inexperienced girl of the upper class. There was nothing to show that it was the work of a beginner. Her faculty for observation is extraordinarily keen, her descriptions of character are terse, striking, and appropriate, and the construction of the piece is clever. It shows a thoughtful mind, and there is none of the clumsy handling noticeable in young writers; the conflict is carefully thought out, and described with mathematical clearness. But however ornate an author's style, however remarkable her intellect, these qualities do not form the most important part of her talent as a woman and an authoress. In considering the first book of a writer who afterwards became celebrated throughout Europe, the question of primary importance is this: How much character is revealed in this book?

Or, to put the question with greater precision, since it concerns a woman: How much character is there that the author was not able to suppress?

The sky seems colored with the deep glow of dawn; it is the great expectancy of love. Here we have the writing of a young girl who knows nothing about love except the one thing,—that it is a woman's whole existence. She has never experienced it, but her active mind has already grasped some of its difficulties; and one great difficulty, which must not be overlooked, is the bourgeois desire to maintain a sure footing. An actress is going to marry into a respectable middle-class family. Nobody in this section of society can think of love otherwise than clad in a white apron and armed with a matronly bunch of keys. Love here means the commonplace. The actress is accustomed to a worse but wider sphere; love for her means to become a great actress, to attain perfection in her art, but to her intended it means that she should love him and keep house.

The problem does not often present itself like this in real life, and if it did the result would in all probability be very different; in the imagination of a well-bred girl of eighteen, like Anne Charlotte Leffler, it was the only conclusion possible. And as he will not consent to her wishes, and she refuses to give way to his; as he has no desire to marry an actress, and she no intention of becoming a housewife, they separate with mutual promises of eternal platonic love.

The end is comic, but it is meant to be taken seriously. No matter how it begins, the ordinary woman's book always ends with platonic love; and it is very characteristic of Anne Charlotte Leffler that her first play should have a platonic and not a tragic ending.

The tragic element, which generally assumes supernatural proportions in the imagination of the young, did not appeal to her; her life was placed in comfortable, bourgeois surroundings, and she was perfectly contented with it.

We find the same want of imagination in all the Swedish authoresses, from Fru Lenngren, Frederica Bremer, and Fru Flygare-Carlén onwards.

A few years later Anne Charlotte Leffler wrote a three-act play, called "The Elf," of which the two first acts afford the best possible key to her own psychology. It was acted for the first time in 1881, but it was probably written soon after her marriage, in 1872, with Edgren, who was at that time in the service of the government.

4

Fru Edgren was one of those proud, straightforward women who would never dream of allowing any one to commiserate them. She made no attempt to suit her actions to please the world; her sole ambition was to show herself as she really was. When she wished to do a thing, she did it as quickly as possible, and without any one's help. She wrote under the influence of her personal impressions, her personal judgment, and her personal opinions; whatever she might attain to in the future, she was determined to have no one but herself to thank for it. But she was a woman. Though usually possessed of a clear judgment, she did not sufficiently realize what it means for a woman to enter upon a literary career by herself. She succeeded in her literary career; but in doing so she sacrificed the best part of her life, and was obliged to suppress her best and truest aspirations, thereby destroying a large amount of real artistic talent.

There are few things that afford me more genuine pleasure than the books of modern authors. I enjoy them less on account of what they tell me than for that which they have been unable to conceal. When they write their books, they write the history of their inner life. You open a book and you read twenty lines, and in the tone and character of those twenty lines you seem to feel the beating of the writer's pulse. In the same way as a fine musical ear can distinguish a single false note in an orchestra, a fine psychological instinct can discern the true from the false, and can tell where the author describes his own feelings and where he is only pretending—can discern his true character from among the multitude of conscious and unconscious masks, and can say: This is good metal, and that a worthless composition, wherewith he makes a dupe of himself and of others.

The woman who attempts to write without a man to shield her, to throw a protecting arm around her, is an unfortunate, incongruous being. That which sets her soul aglow—which calls loudly within her— she dare not say. When a man wishes to be a great writer, he defies conventionalism and compels it to become subservient to him; but for a lonely woman, conventionalism is her sole support, not only out-wardly, but inwardly also. It forms a part of her womanly modesty; it is the guide of her life, from which naught but love can free her; that is why the more talented a woman is, the more absolutely love must be her pilot.

Fru Edgren's best play and her two most interesting stories are "The Elf," "Aurora Bunge," and "Love and Womanhood." None of her other works can be said to equal these in depth of feeling, and none strike a more melancholy note. There is an emotional, nervous life in them which presents an attractive contrast to the cold irony of her other works. She has put her whole being into these writings, with something of her womanly power to charm; while in the others we meet with the clear insight, the critical faculty, and the rare sarcasm to which they owe their reputation.

Yet in these three works we notice how very much she is hedged in on all sides by conventionalism. "The Elf," "Love and Womanhood," and "Aurora Bunge" make us think of a large and beautiful bird that cannot fly because its long, swift wings have been broken by a fall from the nest.

The "elf" is the wife of the respected mayor of a small country town. Her father was a Swedish artist, whose whole life was spent in travelling, because every time that he came home he was driven away by the narrow social life of Sweden. When he is lying on his deathbed, he leaves his penniless child to the care of his younger friend, the Mayor, who knows no better way of providing for her than by making her his wife. He is universally considered the best son, the best partner in business, and the best man—in the town. The elf wanders about the woods, and becomes the subject of much gossip, likewise of envy, among the smart ladies of the town.

One evening when they are giving a party, and she forgets to play the part of hostess, their neighbor, a Baron, arrives with his sister. Both, no longer young, free from illusions, liberal in thought and speech, seem to carry with them a breath from a bigger world; their mere presence serves to make the elf thoughtlessly happy, and from henceforward she sits daily to the Baron for a picture representing Undine when the knight carries her through the wood, and her soul awakes within her. The elf's soul—*i.e.*, love—is also awakened. She feels herself drawn towards this man, who has sufficient fire to awaken her womanhood with a kiss. She does not wish, she does not think, but she would not like to be separated from him; he lives in an atmosphere that suits her, and in which she thrives. She is still a child; but the child would like to wake. It is true that her conscience reproaches her with regard to the Mayor, but here the circumstances are related as though she were not quite married,—that is a mistake which nearly all Teutonic authoresses make.

The Baron tells her the story of Undine. The knight finds her at the moment when the brook stretches forth his long white arm to draw her back, but he does not let her go; he takes her in his arms and carries her away, and she looks up at him with a half anxious expression—there is something new in this expression. She is no longer Undine. She loves. She has a soul.

In this drama, Anne Charlotte Edgren-Leffler, the future leader of the woman's rights movement, makes the confession that a woman's soul is—love. She is the only Swedish woman writer who would have owned as much.

The Baron is a decadent. Fru Edgren took this type from real life long before the decadence made its appearance in literature. He had enjoyed all sensations with delight and inner emotion, until the woman in the elf opens her eyes in the first moment of half consciousness, and when that happens she becomes indifferent to him. His passion cools. It is true that his actions still tend in the same direction, but he is able to gaze at his thoughts critically. He is not the knight who lifts Undine out of the cold water. He leaves her lying in the brook.

Among the experiences by means of which "independent" women, with a "vocation," awake to womanhood, this is probably the most common. It is very difficult to define their feelings when they realize a change in the man who first aroused their affections; but I think that I am not far wrong in saying that it is something akin to loathing. The more sensitive the woman, and the more innocent she is, the longer the loathing will last. However cold her outward behavior may appear, the feeling is still there.

There is nothing that a woman resents more keenly than when a man plays with her affections, and neglects her afterwards. The more inexperienced the woman, the more unmanly this behavior seems. If she is a true woman, her disappointment will be all the greater; she will feel it not only with regard to this single individual, but it will cast a shadow over all men.

The last act reveals the author's perplexity. From an esthetic point of view the ending is cold, and to a certain extent indifferently executed; but judged from a psychological point of view, it is thoroughly Swedish. Considered as the writing of a young lady in the year 1880, it must be confessed that the dialogue is tolerably strong, even *piquante*; but in order to please the highly respected public, it is necessary for the play to end well.

Suddenly they one and all—in this land of pietism and sudden conversion—beat their breasts and confess their sins. The Mayor examines himself, and repents that he was selfish enough to marry the elf; his mother repents because she cared more for her son than her daughter-in-law; the elf repents because she almost allowed herself to be betrayed into falling in love; and the Baron's sister, who, throughout the piece, has always held aloft the banner of love and liberty, repents in a general way, without any particular reason being given. Thus everything returns to its former condition, and Undine remains in the duck-pond.

With this satisfying termination, "The Elf" survived a large number of performances.

The question which suggests itself to my mind is: Whether the author intended the piece to end in this manner? Or was the original ending less conventional, and was Fru Edgren obliged to alter it in order that the play might be acted? What else could she do? A lonely woman like her dared not sin against the public morals. It were better to sin against anything else, only not against the public morals; for in that case they would have condemned her to silence, and her career would have been at an end. The keynote of the piece was the yearning to escape from the long Swedish winters and the gossip by the fireside, out into the fresh air, into the light and warmth of the South.

5

Ten years afterwards Fru Edgren returned to the same problem in "Love and Womanhood," and this time she treated it with greater delicacy and more depth of feeling.

The heroine is no longer the traditional elf, but the modern girl,—nervous, sensitive, with a sharp intellect and still sharper tongue; she is very critical, very reserved, full of secret aspirations, and very warm-hearted; her heart is capable of becoming a world to the man she loves, but it needs a man's love to develop its power of loving. She loves an elegant, self-satisfied Swedish lieutenant, who has served as a volunteer in Algiers, and has written a book on military science; he is just an ordinary smart young man, and he takes it for granted that she will accept him the instant he proposes. But she refuses him. He is indignant and hurt; he cannot understand it at all, unless she loves some one else. But no, she does not love any one else. Then what is the reason? She is sure that he does not care enough for her; there is such an indescribable difference between her love for him, or rather the love that she knows herself capable of feeling, and the affection that he has to offer her, that she will not have him on any account, and looks upon his proposal almost in the light of an insult. He goes away, and returns, soon afterwards, engaged to a little goose.

Fru Edgren develops an elaborate theory, to which she returns again and again. According to her, it is only the commonplace little girls of eighteen, innocence in a white pinafore, with whom men fall in love. I myself do not think that there is much in it: a dozen men who are non-entities fall in love with a dozen young women who are likewise nonentities. On the other hand, we have that numerous type, which includes the modern girl, full of soul, originality, and depth of character, clever and modest, possessed of a keen divination with regard to her own feelings and that of others, mingled with a chaste pride that is founded upon the consciousness of her own importance,—a pride that will not accept less than it gives. And these girls are confined to the narrow circle to which all women are reduced, to two or three possibilities in the whole course of their long youth, possibilities which chance throws in their way, and which are perhaps no possibilities at all to them. A few years pass by, and these girls have become stern judges upon the rights of love, and they have developed a bitter expression about the mouth, and a secret gnawing in the soul. A few years more, and this unappreciated womanly instinct will have brought them to hate men.

Fru Edgren went the same way. In her "Sketches from Life" we find some traces of this feeling in the stories where she displays the comparative worth of men and women; take, for instance, the tale called "At War with Society." But before she had quite joined the army of stern judges, she weighed the problem of love once more, in the second of her five completed novels, called, "Aurora Bunge."

For the last ten years Aurora Bunge has been chief among the ball beauties of Stockholm. Everything in her life is arranged and settled beforehand. In the winter she goes to balls, night after night, to parties and plays; in the summer she is occupied in much the same way in a fashionable watering-place. For the last ten years she has known exactly with whom she is going to dance, what compliments will be paid her, what offers she will receive, and whom she is eventually going to marry. The marriage can be put off until she is thirty—and now she is nearly thirty, and the time has come. She is one of those girls who have danced and danced until everything has grown equally indifferent and wearisome to them; and yet she is without experience, and is likely to remain so to the end. She allows herself perfect freedom of speech, but she will never allow herself a single free action. A couple of intrigues in the dim future are not entirely excluded from her plans, but what difference will that make? She has something of Strindberg's "Julie," but without the latter's perversity; she is also some years in advance of her. She would have no objection to eloping with a circus rider, or doing something *de très mauvais goût*, but she knows that she will never do it. The summer previous to the announcement of her engagement she is seized with a fit of liking the country, and she accompanies her mother to one of her properties, which is situated on a desolate part of the coast. It is the first of her thirty summer visits that is not quite *comme il faut*. In a sudden outburst of enthusiasm for nature, she spends days and weeks wandering about in the woods and fields, with torn dress and down-trodden shoes, and goes out sailing with the fishermen. She becomes stronger and more beautiful, and is more than ever imbued with an indescribable longing. This vague longing leads her on towards that which she is going to experience—which is to be her life's only experience. She feels her pulses beat and her heart burn within her, and not till then does the matured woman of thirty tear aside the bandage that binds her eyes; and looking out, she cries: Where art thou, who givest me life's fulness? On one of her boating expeditions, she goes to the nearest lighthouse. The lighthouse-keeper, a strong, quiet young man, comes out. She looks, and she knows that it is he!

Up to this point Fru Edgren has copied the secret writing in her own soul, and every touch is true. But her experience went no further. The part that follows is psychological and logical too, but it has the greatest fault that a romance can have; *i.e.*, it is word for word imagined, not experienced, and for this reason it is overdrawn. Aurora has scarcely landed before a storm sets in. She flutters like an exhausted bird, in and out of the narrow lighthouse. The lighthouse-keeper sees the danger, and hurries down. She wants to throw herself into the water. He climbs down the rocks and seizes hold of her. Already before, this son of the people had found time to give her a love poem to read. The storm lasts three days, and for three days she remains there. On the fourth day the fishermen return to fetch her, and the lighthouse-keeper is furious. By this time she is no better than a very ordinary fisher girl. She is deathly pale, but insists on leaving him. He threatens her with his fists, and she proposes that they should drown themselves together; but his mother had already drowned herself, and he does not wish to have two suicides in the family. Aurora goes home, and they never meet again. A few months afterwards she marries an officer who is in debt.

Fru Edgren's men may be divided into two types,—the one she cannot endure, but she describes him admirably; the other she cannot describe at all, but she likes him very much indeed. The first is the fashionable man of Stockholm society, who has tasted life's pleasures, and is wearied of them; the second is the simple, unsophisticated son of the people.

6

Fru Edgren looked life boldly in the face.—life, which was continually passing her by, because she was a lady, whose duty it was to lead a blameless existence. She was by this time a celebrated authoress, with a comfortable income, but what had she gained by it? Merely this: that envious eyes watched her more narrowly than before, and that she was expected to live for the honor and glory of Sweden, and for the honor and glory of her position as a woman writer. Yet, after all, were they not in the North? And was she not allowed all possible freedom up to a certain point? Even this certain point might be overstepped sometimes,—in private, of course,—and such was the general usage. But she was one of those proud natures who will not tolerate a greasy fingermark on the untarnished shield of their honor, and she was also one of those sovereign natures whose will is a law to themselves.

We are confronted by a strange sight in Scandinavian literature. We find man's laxity and woman's prudery existing side by side. Björnson, Ibsen, Garborg, Strindberg, were contemporaries of Fru Edgren, and their renown was at its height. The eighties were the great period of Scandinavian romance, and this romance turned solely upon the problem of man and woman. The productive enthusiasm of those days drove a multitude of women into the fields of literature, including those whom we have mentioned, who died early, and some lesser ones, who still continue to lead a useless, literary existence. But their writings are strangely poor compared with those of the men, even though there were numbered amongst them an Edgren-Leffler, an Ahlgren, and a Kovalevsky. The men were not afraid; they all had something to impart, and that which they imparted was themselves. But there was not a single woman's voice to join in the mighty chorus of the hymn to love; not one of them had experienced it, and they had nothing to say. Their longing kept silence. When, however, the literature of indignation, with Kalchas Björnson at its head, broke loose against the corruptions and depravity of men, then all the authoresses raised their voices, and instituted a grand inquisition.

Fru Edgren took part in it. What hymn could she sing? She had no experience of love, and her patience was at an end. Towards the end of the eighties, love had completely vanished from her books, and its place had been filled by the question of rights,—women's rights with regard to property and wage-earning, and marriage rights. "The Doll's

House" was followed by a deluge of books on unhappy marriages, and Fru Edgren contributed to increase their number. In a play called "True Women," she contrasts the hard-working, wage-earning woman with the indolent, extravagant man; while she severely condemns the woman who so far lowers herself as to love a husband who has been unfaithful to her. She is, in fact, so badly disposed towards love that she allows an honest, hard-working man, in the same piece, to be refused by an honest, hard-working woman, and for the simple reason that superior people must no longer propose, nor allow others to propose to them.

Her drama, "How People do Good," is written in the same mood. "The Gauntlet" and "The Doll's House" have exerted such a great influence over her that she has unconsciously quoted whole sentences. She has become no better than the ordinary platform woman; her former sense and good taste are no longer to be observed in her writings, and even socialism has a place in her program. This woman, who knows nothing of the proletarian, represents him in a melodramatic manner, as she has done before with the son of the people. She travels about the country and fights for her rights; she becomes a propagandist.

It was at this time that the celebrated mathematician, Sonia Kovalevsky, was appointed to the high school at Stockholm at the instigation of Fru Edgren's brother, Professor Mittag-Leffler, and the two women became the greatest of friends. Sonia Kovalevsky had practiced the principles of women's rights and asceticism in her own married life, and was now, after her husband had shot himself, a widow.

She was probably Björnson's model in more than one of his books, and she combined Russian fanaticism with the Russian capacity to please. She had not been long at Stockholm before the war broke loose. Strindberg raged against women, ignoring Fru Edgren and others on the plea that they could not be reckoned as women, since they had no children. Björnson and Fru Edgren were everywhere welcomed at women's meetings as the champions of women's rights.

For four or five years Sonia Kovalevsky and Fru Edgren were almost inseparable. Fru Edgren took back her maiden name of Leffler after her separation from her husband. The two friends were always travelling. They went to Norway, France, England, etc., together, and Fru Leffler wrote her longest novel, "A Tale of Summer." It was the old problem of love and the artistic temperament. A highly gifted artist falls in love with a commonplace schoolmaster,—she nervous, refined, independent; he young, big, strong, true-hearted, and very like a trusty Newfoundland dog. It does not answer. An artist must not marry, the most learned of Newfoundland dogs cannot understand an artist, and yet artists have a most unfortunate preference for Newfoundland dogs.

There was something in this novel that was not to be found in any of her earlier works,—a hasty, uneven beat of the pulse, something of the fever of awakened passion.

Sonia, meantime, was engaged with her work for the *Prix Bordin*; but she had scarcely begun her studies before she left them to devote herself to a parallel romance, about which she was very much excited. It was called "The Struggle for Happiness: How it Was, and How it Might Have Been." She persuaded Fru Leffler to give this thought a dramatic setting, and she was very anxious to have it published. It was nothing more or less than a hymn to love, which had fast begun to set flame to her ungovernable Russian blood. Fru Leffler wrote the piece, but it proved an utter failure.

On her travels she made the acquaintance of the Duke of Cajanello, a mathematician, who was probably introduced to her by Sonia Kovalevsky He was professor at the Lyceum at Naples, and Fru Leffler appears to have fallen suddenly and passionately in love. Her last novel bears witness to this fact; like the former one, it treats of "Love and Womanhood," but here the proof of true womanliness lies in the loving. She was divorced from her husband and went to Italy. Liberty, love, and the South,—all were hers at last.

She had something else besides to satisfy her ambition as a society lady, when, in May, 1890, she became the Duchess of Cajanello. After her marriage she paid a visit to Stockholm with her husband, and every one thought that she looked younger, more gentle, more womanly, and happier than she had ever done before.

After the marriage, her friendship with Sonia Kovalevsky was at an end. The latter had not found happiness in loving, and she died in the year 1891.

The Duchess of Cajanello lived at Naples, and in her forty-third year she experienced for the first time the happiness of becoming a mother. When she died, the little duke was scarcely more than six months old. Up to the last few days of her life, she was to all appearances happy and in good health. Her last work was the life of her friend Sonia Kovalevsky. In writing it she fulfilled the promise which they had made, that whichever of the two survived should write the life—a living portrait it was to be—of the other. She had just begun to correct the proofs before she died. On the last day before her illness, she worked till three o'clock in the afternoon at a novel called "A Narrow Horizon," which was left unfinished. She died after a few days' illness.

Fru Edgren-Leffler belonged to that class of women whose senses slumber long because their vital strength gives them the expectation of long youth. But when the day comes that they are awakened, the same vitality that had kept them asleep overflows with an intensity that attracts like a beacon on a dark night. It is the woman who attracts the man, not the reverse. Fru Edgren-Leffler found in her fortieth year that which she had sought for in vain in her twentieth and thirtieth,—love! The unfruitful became fruitful; the emaciated became beautiful; the woman's rights woman sang a hymn to the mystery of love; and the last short years of happiness, too soon interrupted by death, were a contradiction to the long insipid period of literary production.

THE END

The Keynotes Series.

16mo. Cloth. Each volume with a Titlepage and Cover Design.
By AUBREY BEARDSLEY.
Price $1.00.

*****

I. KEYNOTES. By George Egerton.

II. THE DANCING FAUN. By Florence Farr.

III. POOR FOLK. By Fedor Dostoievsky. Translated from the Russian by Lena Milman. With an Introduction by George Moore.

IV. A CHILD OF THE AGE. By Francis Adams.

V. THE GREAT GOD PAN AND THE INMOST LIGHT. By Arthur Machen.

VI. DISCORDS. By George Egerton.

VII. PRINCE ZALESKI. By M. P. Shiel.

VIII. THE WOMAN WHO DID. By Grant Allen.

IX. *WOMEN'S TRAGEDIES. By H. D. Lowry.*

X. *GREY ROSES AND OTHER STORIES. By Henry Harland.*

XI. *AT THE FIRST CORNER AND OTHER STORIES. By H. B. Marriott Watson.*

XII. *MONOCHROMES. By Ella D'arcy.*

XIII. *AT THE RELTON ARMS. By Evelyn Sharp.*

XIV. *THE GIRL FROM THE FARM. By Gertrude Dix.*

XV. *THE MIRROR OF MUSIC. By Stanley V. Makower.*

XVI. *YELLOW AND WHITE. By W. Carlton Dawe.*

XVII. *THE MOUNTAIN LOVERS. By Fiona Macleod.*

XVIII. *THE THREE IMPOSTORS. By Arthur Machen.*

Sold by all Booksellers. Mailed, postpaid, on receipt of price, by the Publishers,
ROBERTS BROTHERS, Boston, Mass.
John Lane, The Bodley Head, Vigo Street, London, W.

*****

Messrs. Roberts Brothers' Publications.
Foam of the Sea.
By GERTRUDE HALL,
Author of "Far from To-day," "Allegretto," "Verses," etc.
16mo. Cloth. Price, $1.00.

*****

Miss Gertrude Hall's second volume of short stories, "Foam of the Sea and Other Tales," shows the same characteristics as the first, which will be instantly remembered under the title of "Far from To-day." They are vigorous, fanciful, in part quaint, always thought-stirring and thoughtful. She has followed old models somewhat in her style, and the setting of many of the tales is medieval. The atmosphere of them is fascinating, so unusual and so pervading is it; and always refined are her stories, and graceful, even with an occasional touch of grotesquerie. And there is an underlying subtleness in them, a grasp of the problems of the heart and the head, in short, of life, which is remarkable; and yet they, for the most part, are romantic to a high degree, and reveal an imagination far beyond the ordinary. "Foam of the Sea," like "Far from To-day," is a volume of rare tales, beautifully wrought out of the past for the delectation of the present.

Of the six tales in the volume, "Powers of Darkness" alone has a wholly nineteenth century flavor. It is a sermon told through two lives pathetically miserable. "The Late Returning" is dramatic and admirably turned, strong in its heart analysis. "Foam of the Sea" is almost archaic in its rugged simplicity, and "Garden Deadly" (the most imaginative of the six) is beautiful in its descriptions, weird in its setting, and curiously effective. "The Wanderers" is a touching tale of the early Christians, and "In Battlereagh House" there is the best character drawing.

Miss Hall is venturing along a unique line of story telling, and must win the praise of the discriminating.—*The Boston Times.*

There is something in the quality of the six stories by Gertrude Hall in the volume to which this title is given which will attract attention. They are stories which must—some of them—be read more than once to be appreciated. They are fascinating in their subtlety of suggestion, in their keen analysis of motive, and in their exquisite grace of diction. There is great dramatic power in "Powers of Darkness" and "In

Battlereagh House." They are stories which should occupy more than the idle hour. They are studies.—*Boston Advertiser.*

She possesses a curious originality, and, what does not always accompany this rare faculty, skill in controlling it and compelling it to take artistic forms.—*Mail and Express.*

*****

Sold by all Booksellers. Mailed, postpaid, on receipt of price, by the Publishers, ROBERTS BROTHERS, Boston, Mass.

*****

FAR FROM TO-DAY. A Volume of Stories.
By GERTRUDE HALL,
16mo. Cloth. Price, $1.00.

THESE stories are marked with originality and power. The titles are as follows: viz., Tristiane, The Sons of Philemon, Servirol, Sylvanus, Theodolind, Shepherds.

Miss Hall has put together here a set of gracefully written tales,—tales of long ago. They have an old-world medieval feeling about them, soft with intervening distance, like the light upon some feudal castle wall, seen through the openings of the forest. A refined fancy and many an artistic touch has been spent upon the composition with good result.—*London Bookseller.*

"Although these six stories are dreams of the misty past, their morals have a most direct bearing on the present. An author who has the soul to conceive such stories is worthy to rank among the highest. One of our best literary critics, Mrs. Louise Chandler Moulton, says: 'I think it is a work of real genius, Homeric in its simplicity, and beautiful exceedingly.'"

Mrs. Harriet Prescott Spofford, in the *Newburyport Herald:*—

"A volume giving evidence of surprising genius is a collection of six tales by Gertrude Hall, called 'Far from To-day.' I recall no stories at once so powerful and subtle as these. Their literary charm is complete, their range of learning is vast, and their human interest is intense. 'Tristiane,' the first one, is as brilliant and ingenious, to say the least, as the best chapter of Arthur Hardy's 'Passe Rose:' 'Sylvanus' tells a heart-breaking tale, full of wild delight in hills and winds and skies, full of pathos and poetry; in 'The Sons of Philemon' the Greek spirit is perfect, the story absolutely beautiful; 'Theodolind,' again, repeats the Norse life to the echo, even to the very measure of the runes; and 'The Shepherds' gives another reading to the meaning of 'The Statue and the Bust.' Portions of these stories are told with an almost archaic simplicity, while other portions mount on great wings of poetry, 'Far from To-day,' as the time of the stories is placed; the hearts that beat in them are the hearts of to-day, and each one of these stories breathes the joy and the sorrow of life, and is rich with the beauty of the world."

From the *London Academy*, December 24th:—

"The six stories in the dainty volume entitled 'Far from To-day' are of imagination all compact. The American short tales, which have of late attained a wide and deserved popularity in this country, have not been lacking in this vitalizing quality; but the art of Mrs. Slosson and Miss Wilkins is that of imaginative realism, while that of Miss Gertrude Hall is that of imaginative romance; theirs is the work of impassioned observation, hers of impassioned invention. There is in her book a fine, delicate fantasy that reminds one of Hawthorne in his sweetest moods; and while Hawthorne had certain gifts which were all his own, the new writer exhibits a certain winning tenderness in which he was generally deficient. In the domain of pure romance it is long since we have had anything so rich in simple beauty as is the work which is to be found between the covers of 'Far from To-day.'"

*****

Sold by all Booksellers. Mailed, postpaid, on receipt of price, by the Publishers,
ROBERTS BROTHERS, Boston, Mass.

*****

THE WEDDING GARMENT.
A Tale of the Life to Come.
BY LOUIS PENDLETON.

*****

16mo. Cloth, price, $1.00. White and gold, $1.25.

*****

"The Wedding Garment" tells the story of the continued existence of a young man after his death or departure from the natural world. Awakening in the other world,—in an intermediate region between Heaven and Hell, where the good and the evil live together temporarily commingled,—he is astonished and delighted to find himself the same man in all respects as to every characteristic of his mind and ultimate of the body. So closely does everything about him resemble the world he has left behind, that he believes he is still in the latter until convinced of the error. The young man has good impulses, but is no saint, and he listens to the persuasions of certain persons who were his friends in the world, but who are now numbered among the evil, even to the extent of following them downward to the very confines of Hell. Resisting at last and saving himself, later on, and after many remarkable experiences, he gradually makes his way through the intermediate region to the gateways of Heaven,—which can be found only by those prepared to enter,—where he is left with the prospect before him of a blessed eternity in the company of the woman he loves.

The book is written in a reverential spirit, it is unique and quite unlike any story of the same type heretofore published, full of telling incidents and dramatic situations, and not merely a record of the doings of sexless "shades" but of *living* human beings.

The one grand practical lesson which this book teaches, and which is in accord with the divine Word and the New Church unfoldings of it everywhere teach, is the need of an interior, true purpose in life. The deepest ruling purpose which we cherish, what we constantly strive for and determine to pursue as the most real and precious thing of life, that rules us everywhere, that is our ego, our life, is what will have its way at last. It will at last break through all disguise; it will bring all external conduct into harmony with itself. If it be an evil and selfish end, all external and fair moralities will melt away, and the man will lose his common sense and exhibit his insanities of opinion and will and answering deed on the surface. But if that end be good and innocent, and there be humility within, the outward disorders and evils which result from one's heredity or surroundings will finally disappear.—*From Rev. John Goddard's discourse, July 1, 1894.*

Putting aside the question as to whether the scheme of the soul's development after death was or was not revealed to Swedenborg, whether or not the title of seer can be added to the claims of this learned student of science, all this need not interfere with the moral influence of this work, although the weight of its instruction must be greatly enforced on the minds of those who believe in a later inspiration than the gospels.

This story begins where others end; the title of the first chapter, "I Die," commands attention; the process of the soul's disenthralment is certainly in harmony with what we sometimes read in the dim eyes of friends we follow to the very gate of life. "By what power does a single spark hold to life so long ... this lingering of the divine spark of life in a body growing cold?" It is the mission of the author to tear from Death its long-established thoughts of horror, and upon its entrance into a new life, the soul possesses such a power of adjustment that no shock is experienced.—*Boston Transcript.*

*****

ROBERTS BROTHERS, Publishers,
BOSTON, MASS.

*****

POOR FOLK.
A Novel.
Translated from the Russian of Fedor Dostoievsky, by Lena Milman, with decorative titlepage and a critical introduction by George Moore. American Copyright edition.
16mo. Cloth. $1.00.

*****

A capable critic writes: "One of the most beautiful, touching stories I have read. The character of the old clerk is a masterpiece, a kind of Russian Charles Lamb. He reminds me, too, of Anatole France's 'Sylvestre Bonnard,' but it is a more poignant, moving figure. How wonderfully, too, the sad little strokes of humor are blended into the pathos in his characterization, and how fascinating all the naive self-revelations of his poverty become,—all his many ups and downs and hopes and fears. His unsuccessful visit to the money-lender, his despair at the office, unexpectedly ending in a sudden burst of good fortune, the final despairing cry of his love for Varvara,—these hold one breathless. One can hardly read them without tears.... But there is no need to say all that could be said about the book. It is enough to say that it is over powerful and beautiful."

We are glad to welcome a good translation of the Russian Dostoievsky's story "Poor Folk," Englished by Lena Milman. It is a tale of unrequited love, conducted in the form of letters written between a poor clerk and his girl cousin whom he devotedly loves, and who finally leaves him to marry a man not admirable in character who, the reader feels, will not make her happy. The pathos of the book centers in the clerk, Makar's, unselfish affection and his heart-break at being left lonesome by his charming kinswoman whose epistles have been his one solace. In the conductment of the story, realistic sketches of middle-class Russian life are given, heightening the effect of the denoument. George Moore writes a sparkling introduction to the book.—*Hartford Courant.*

Dostoievsky is a great artist. "Poor Folk" is a great novel.—*Boston Advertiser.*

It is a most beautiful and touching story, and will linger in the mind long after the book is closed. The pathos is blended with touching bits of humor, that are even pathetic in themselves.—*Boston Times.*

Notwithstanding that "Poor Folk" is told in that most exasperating and entirely unreal style—by letters—it is complete in sequence, and the interest does not flag as the various phases in the sordid life of the two characters are developed. The theme is intensely pathetic and truly human, while its treatment is exceedingly artistic. The translator, Lena Milman, seems to have well preserved the spirit of the original.—*Cambridge Tribune.*

*****

ROBERTS BROTHERS, Publishers,
BOSTON, MASS.

*****

THE WOMAN WHO DID.
BY GRANT ALLEN.
Keynotes Series. American Copyright Edition.
16mo. Cloth. Price, $1.00.

*****

A very remarkable story, which in a coarser hand than its refined and gifted author could never have been effectively told; for such a hand could not have sustained the purity of motive, nor have portrayed the noble, irreproachable character of Herminia Barton.—*Boston Home Journal.*

"The Woman Who Did" is a remarkable and powerful story. It increases our respect for Mr. Allen's ability, nor do we feel inclined to join in throwing stones at him as a perverter of our morals and our social institutions. However widely we may differ from Mr. Allen's views on many important questions, we are bound to recognize his sincerity, and to respect him accordingly. It is powerful and painful, but it is not convincing. Herminia Barton is a woman whose nobleness both of mind and of life we willingly concede; but as she is presented to us by Mr. Allen, there is unmistakably a flaw in her intellect. This in itself does not detract from the reality of the picture.—*The Speaker.*

In the work itself, every page, and in fact every line, contains outbursts of intellectual passion that places this author among the giants of the nineteenth century.—*American Newsman.*

Interesting, and at times intense and powerful.—*Buffalo Commercial.*

No one can doubt the sincerity of the author.—*Woman's Journal.*

The story is a strong one, very strong, and teaches a lesson that no one has a right to step aside from the moral path laid out by religion, the law, and society.—*Boston Times.*

*****

Sold by all Booksellers. Mailed, postpaid, on receipt of price, by the Publishers,
ROBERTS BROTHERS, Boston, Mass.

*****

DISCORDS.
A Volume of Stories.
By GEORGE EGERTON, author of "Keynotes."
AMERICAN COPYRIGHT EDITION.
16mo. Cloth. Price, $1.00.

George Egerton's new volume entitled "Discords," a collection of short stories, is more talked about, just now, than any other fiction of the day. The collection is really stories for story-writers. They are precisely the quality which literary folk will wrangle over. Harold Frederic cables from London to the "New York Times" that the book is making a profound impression there. It is published on both sides, the Roberts House bringing it out in Boston. George Egerton, like George Eliot and George Sand, is a woman's *nom de plume.* The extraordinary frankness with which life in general is discussed in these stories not unnaturally arrests attention.—*Lilian Whiting.*

The English woman, known as yet only by the name of George Egerton, who made something of a stir in the world by a volume of strong stories called "Keynotes," has brought out a new book under the rather uncomfortable title of "Discords." These stories show us pessimism run wild; the gloomy things that can happen to a human being are so dwelt upon as to leave the impression that in the author's own world there is no light. The relations of the sexes are treated of in bitter irony, which develops into actual horror as the pages pass. But in all this there is a rugged grandeur of style, a keen analysis of motive, and a deepness of pathos that stamp George Egerton as one of the greatest women writers of the day. "Discords" has been called a volume of stories; it is a misnomer, for the book contains merely varying episodes in lives of men and women, with no plot, no beginning nor ending.—*Boston Traveller.*

This is a new volume of psychological stories from the pen and brains of George Egerton, the author of "Keynotes." Evidently the titles of the author's books are selected according to musical principles. The first story in the book is "A Psychological Moment at Three Periods." It is all strength rather than sentiment. The story of the child, of the girl, and of the woman is told, and told by one to whom the mysteries of the life of each are familiarly known. In their very truth, as the writer has so subtly analyzed her triple characters, they sadden one to think that such things must be; yet as they are real, they are bound to be disclosed by somebody and in due time. The author betrays remarkable penetrative skill and perception, and dissects the human heart with a power from whose demonstration the sensitive nature may instinctively shrink even while fascinated with the narration and hypnotized by the treatment exhibited.—*Courier.*

*****

Sold by all Booksellers. Mailed by Publishers,
ROBERTS BROTHERS, Boston, Mass.

*****

Balzac in English.

*****

Memoirs of Two Young Married Women.
By Honoré de Balzac.
Translated by Katharine Prescott Wormeley. 12mo. Half Russia. Price, $1.50.

*****

"There are," says Henry James in one of his essays, "two writers in Balzac,—the spontaneous one and the reflective one, the former of which is much the more delightful, while the latter is the more extraordinary." It is the reflective Balzac, the Balzac with a theory, whom we get in the "Deux Jeunes Mariées," now translated by Miss Wormeley under the title of "Memoirs of Two Young Married Women." The theory of Balzac is that the marriage of convenience, properly regarded, is far preferable to the marriage simply from love, and he undertakes to prove this proposition by contrasting the careers of two young girls who have been fellow-students at a convent. One of them, the ardent and passionate Louise de Chaulieu, has an intrigue with a Spanish refugee, finally marries him, kills him, as she herself confesses, by her perpetual jealousy and exaction, mourns his loss bitterly, then marries a golden-haired youth, lives with him in a dream of ecstasy for a year or so, and this time kills herself through jealousy wrongfully inspired. As for her friend, Renée de Maucombe, she dutifully makes a marriage to please her parents, calculates coolly beforehand how many children she will have and how they shall be trained; insists, however, that the marriage shall be merely a civil contract till she and her husband find that their hearts are indeed one; and sees all her brightest visions realized—her Louis an ambitious man for her sake and her children truly adorable creatures. The story, which is told in the form of letters, fairly scintillates with brilliant sayings, and is filled with eloquent discourses concerning the nature of love, conjugal and otherwise. Louise and Renée are both extremely sophisticated young women, even in their teens; and those who expect to find in their letters the demure innocence of the

Anglo-Saxon type will be somewhat astonished. The translation, under the circumstances, was rather a daring attempt, but it has been most felicitousy done.—*The Beacon.*

*****

Sold by all booksellers. Mailed, postpaid, on receipt of price by the Publishers,
ROBERTS BROTHERS, Boston, Mass.

*****

GEORGE SAND IN ENGLISH.

*****

NANON.
Translated by ELIZABETH WORMELEY LATIMER.

*****

It is, I think, one of the prettiest and most carefully constructed of her later works, and the best view of the French Revolution from a rural point of view that I know.—*Translator.*

"Nanon" is a pure romance, chaste in style and with a charm of sentiment well calculated to appeal to the most thoughtful reader. George Sand has chosen the epoch of the French Revolution as the scene of this last theme from her prolific pen, and she invests the time with all the terrible significance that belongs to it. To the literary world nothing that comes from her pen is unwelcome, the more so as in this instance there is not the least trace of that risky freedom of speech that too often disfigures the best work of the French school of fiction. Nanon will be read with an appreciation of the gifted novelist that is by no means new, and her claim to recognition is made stronger and better by this masterly work. Her admirers—and they will be sure not to miss Nanon—will feel a debt of gratitude to Elizabeth Wormeley Latimer for a translation that preserves so well the clear, flowing style and the lofty thoughts of the original; and the publishers, no less than the reading public, ought to consider themselves fortunate in the choice of so competent a translator.—*The American Hebrew.*

This is among the finest of George Sand's romances, and one who has not made acquaintance with her works would do well to choose it as the introductory volume. It belongs in the list of the best works of that remarkable author, and contains nothing that is objectionable or at all questionable in its moral tone. The scenes are laid among the peasantry of France—simple-hearted, plodding, honest people, who know little or nothing of the causes which are fomenting to bring about the French Revolution. She portrays in clear and forcible language the destitute condition of the rural districts, whose people were ignorant, priest-ridden, and oppressed; and she shows the wretchedness and misery that these poor people were compelled to endure during the progress of the Revolution. The book is one of her masterpieces, by reason of the exquisite delineations of character, the keen and philosophical thought, the purity of inspiration, and the delicacy and refinement of style. Throughout the story there is a freshness and vigor which only one can feel who has lived at some time in close intimacy with fields and woods, and become familiar with the forms, the colors, and the sounds of Nature. The book has been translated by Elizabeth Wormeley Latimer, who has performed her task admirably.—*Public Opinion.*

Mrs. Latimer has achieved marked success in the translation of this charming tale, preserving its purity, its simplicity, and its pastoral beauty.—*Christian Union.*

*****

One volume, 12mo, half Russia, uniform with our edition of "Balzac" and "Sand" novels. Price, $1.50.

ROBERTS BROTHERS, Boston.

*****

A Beautiful Betrothal and Wedding Gift.

THE

Lover's Year-Book of Poetry.

A Collection of Love Poems for Every Day in the Year.

By HORACE P. CHANDLER.

First Series. Vol. I. January to June. Bicolor, $1.25; white and gold, $1.50. Vol. II. July to December. Bicolor, $1.25; white and gold, $1.50.

Second Series. Vol. I. January to June. Bicolor, $1.25; white and gold, $1.50. Vol. II. July to December. Bicolor, $1.25; white and gold, $1.50.

The Poems in the First Series touch upon Love prior to Marriage; those in the Second Series are of Married-Life and Child-Life.

These two beautiful volumes, clad in the white garb which is emblematic of the purity of married love as well as the innocence of childhood, make up a series unique in its plan and almost perfect in its carrying out. It would be impossible to specify any particular poems of the collection for special praise. They have been selected with unerring taste and judgment, and include some of the most exquisite poems in the language. Altogether the four volumes make up a treasure-house of Love poetry unexcelled for sweetness and purity of expression. *Transcript, Boston.*

Mr. Chandler has drawn from many and diverse wells of English poetry of Love, as the list for any month shows. The poetry of passion is not here, but there are many strains of Love such as faithful lovers feel.—*Literary World, Boston.*

We do not hesitate to pronounce it a collection of extraordinary freshness and merit. It is not in hackneyed rhymes that his lovers converse, but in fresh meters from the unfailing fountains.—*Independent, New York.*

Mr. Chandler is catholic in his tastes, and no author of repute has been omitted who could give variety or strength to the work. The children have never been reached in verse in a more comprehensive and connected manner than they are in this book.—*Gazette, Boston.*

A very dainty and altogether bewitching little anthology. For each day in each month of two years (each series covering a year) a poem is given celebrating the emotions that beset the heart of the true lover. The editor has shown his exquisite taste in selection, and his wide and varied knowledge of the literature of English and American poetry. Every poem in these books is a perfect gem of sentiment; either tender, playful, reproachful, or supplicatory in its meaning; there is not a sonnet nor a lyric that one could wish away.—*Beacon, Boston.*

"The selections," says Louise Chandler Moulton, "given us are nearly all interesting, and some of them are not only charming but unhackneyed."—*Herald, Boston.*

A collection of Love poems selected with exquisite judgment from the best known English and American poets of the last three centuries, with a few translations.—*Home Journal, Boston.*

There are many beautiful poems gathered into this treasure-house, and so great is the variety which has been given to the whole that the monotony which would seem to be the necessary accompaniment of the choice of a single theme is overcome.—*Courier, Boston.*

The selections are not fragments, but are for the most part complete poems. Nearly every one of the poems is a literary gem, and they represent nearly all the famous names in poetry.—*Daily Advertiser, Boston.*

Selected with great taste and judgment from a wide variety of sources, and providing a body of verse of the highest order.—*Commercial Advertiser, Buffalo.*

*****

Sold by all booksellers. Mailed on receipt of price, postpaid, by the publishers,

ROBERTS BROTHERS, Boston, Mass.

*****

FOOTNOTES:

[1]Sonia's mother was a German, the daughter of Schubert the astronomer. Marie Bashkirtseff's grandmother was also German, and Fru Leffler was descended from a German family who had settled in Sweden.
[2]"A Doll's House," by Henrik Ibsen.